NATURE
CRAFT

NORTH
LIGHT
BOOKS

ACKNOWLEDGEMENTS

PHOTOGRAPHS:

Ariadne Holland 104(b), 139: Eric Crichton 71; Dorling Kindersley *(The Complete Book of Dried Flowers)* 53(b), *(The Complete Book of Herbs)* 86(br), 177-118, *(The Indoor Garden)* 23, 90(tl,bl), 101, *(The Scented House)* 85; Eaglemoss (Andrew Murray) 47, (Martin Norris) front cover (inset l), 7, 17, 30-31, 37-40, 76, 81-82, 100, (Simon Page-Ritchie 86(bl), (John Suett) 11, 24-25, 50, 83-84, 95-96, 98, 110, 115, 127, 131, (Steve Tanner) front cover (inset br), 15, 16(t), 27, 41-44, 45-46, 55, 56(tl), 62-63, 64, 65-67, 69, 78-80, 87-89, 90(r), 106(b), 113, 119, 121, 122, 124, 134; Garden Picture Library (Linda Burgess) 59, (Gary Rogers) 94; Robert Harding Picture Library front cover (background) 2-3, 6, 28, 60, 68(tr), 92, 120; HarperCollins *(Creative Basket Making/ Lois Walpole)* 129; Annet Held 77; Insight (Michelle Garrett) front cover (inset tr), 72-74, 91, 102-104, 108(b), (Linda Burgess) 99; Di Lewis (Jane Packer's *Flowers for all Seasons: Winter)* 49; Merehurst Publishing *(Arranging Flowers)* 29, 33-36, 48, *(Dried Flowers)* 86(t); Modes et Travaux 9-10, 51, 54(t), 58(bl), 135, 141; Mondadoripress/*Casaviva* 86(c); Photos Horticultural 61; Salamander Books *(Creative Book of Pressed Flowers)* 68(tl,b); Harry Smith Collection 26, 93, 108-109(t); Tony Stone Worldwide 111; Elizabeth Whiting Associates (Di Lewis) 1, 52, 53(t), 54(b), 58(tl,br), 109(b), 125; 100 Idees 12, 13-14, 16(b), 19-22, 58(tr), 97, 105-106(t), 107, 114, 116, 126, 135-138.

ILLUSTRATIONS:

Elisabeth Dowle 32, 43-44, 46-47, 70, 75, 123; Teri Gower/The Gallery 18, 26, 62, 64, 134; John Hutchinson 142; Bill Le Fever 128, 130-132; Tig Sutton 21, 136-137; Donald Thomas 140.

Based on *Creative Hands,* published in the UK
© Eaglemoss Publications Ltd 1993
All rights reserved

First published in the USA in 1993
by North Light Books,
an imprint of F&W Publications Inc.,
1507 Dana Avenue,
Cincinnati, Ohio 45207.

1-800-289-0963

Manufactured in Hong Kong

CONTENTS

CHAPTER I
◇ TAKEN FROM NATURE ◇

CHAPTER II
◇ FLORAL ARRANGEMENTS ◇

CHAPTER III
◇ PRESSED & DRIED FLOWERS ◇

CHAPTER IV

CRAFTED FROM HERBS

CHAPTER V

 # CRAFTED FROM NATURE

CHAPTER I

TAKEN FROM NATURE

◇

Shells

*Sea shells gathered on summer beaches are
often tidied away and forgotten once the holiday is over.
Rather than hide them, bring them out
of your cupboards and use their subtle beauty to
create natural decorations for your home.*

Sea shells are one of Nature's miniature wonders; their range of subtle colours and intricate shapes seems infinite. Whatever their size, their whorled, conical or tide-smoothed forms and the delicate tracery of their patterns makes each one a marvel in its own right.

One of the simplest pleasures of a summer holiday is combing the beach for shells. Even the most unlikely shores will yield a few beautiful specimens which you can display to spectacular effect.

When beachcombing it is tempting to gather everything you find, but always try to choose perfect examples and remember that some are extremely fragile — they may break if they knock against one another.

More exotic foreign shells are often sold in shops and markets by the sea. Here you can often find unusual and inexpensive examples.

Once home, it is a good idea to wash each shell thoroughly in clean water to get rid of any salty deposits. When immersed, the shells reveal the true beauty of their colours, which naturally fade when dry. One of the simplest ways to display your shells is to place them in a large glass storage jar filled with distilled water to conserve their underwater magic.

◁ *A simple, effective use of tiny shells and pebbles is to store them in slim glass containers. Adding distilled water enhances their colour.*

△ *Miniature shelves or old printers' cases make an attractive alternative for displaying slightly larger shells. Glue them to the background felt.*

Collages and pictures

These are easy to make. Simply cover a piece of hardboard with canvas, use an old picture frame without the glass, or a glass-fronted display case. If you have nothing suitable in your home, a visit to a junk shop or market should provide you with plenty of material.

Experiment with your shells before deciding on the final arrangement. Group them in an abstract manner; in whorls of colour or shape, or use them to create a flower or leaf design.

Choose a clear contact adhesive and use it sparingly to glue the shells to the background. Small shells may need to be held in position until they are dry to prevent them rolling over to the wrong side; pins placed on either side hold them in place.

◁ *Exotic shells set in box frames combine with coral fronds to create a pleasing display.*

Varnishing shells

If you want shells to keep their brilliance when dry, coat them with a thin application of varnish.

Most shells will need to be propped in position before they can be varnished so that you can reach all sides. The easiest way to do this is to hammer a series of nails into a block of scrap wood and slip your shells over the top of the nails. If necessary, secure them to the nail heads with plasticine or Blu-tac. This way you have access to the whole surface and they don't need to be moved until they are completely dry. For tiny shells nail varnish will do. Put aside in a dust-free area until dry.

Painting shells

Pale shells can be made more interesting with the addition of a little colour. Thin down some suitable coloured watercolour paint and brush it sparingly over the surface. Finish off with a coat of varnish to give your shells a pastel glow.

Using your shells

There are many ways to use a shell collection — you can make a collage, create a shell picture, design a table centre or simply pile the shells in glass vases or bowls as stylish decorations.

Pearl candle

This pearl-shaped candle is an extremely simple yet charming way to brighten up a dinner table.

You will need
◇ White spherical candle
◇ Two large scallop shells
◇ Thick-stemmed glass
◇ Sand, small shells or gravel

Half-fill the glass with small shells, sand or gravel. Place the scallop shells in the centre, slightly apart. Put the pearl candle in between them.

Decorating with shells

*Find out about shellwork and you will be able to
create beautiful effects to enhance otherwise plain pieces
of furniture. A variety of pretty shells are found on
beaches and can be used to fantastic effect with the simple
techniques of shellwork.*

Shellwork is a fascinating craft that can be used to transform many plain household items, from small boxes, picture and mirror frames to larger items such as chairs and tables, into original works of art. The craft was a favourite pastime for Victorian ladies who excelled at gluing shells on to surfaces in all sorts of informal or carefully worked out arrangements.

The more types of shells that you can find — from small winkles to large scallops — the more effective the finished item will be. And bear in mind that it's often possible to get large, unusual shells from a local fishmonger. Rather than leave the shells in their natural hues, some or all of them may be coloured to complement the decor of a room or to give an exotic effect.

▽ *The round shell frame of this mirror is easy and fun to make and will serve as an enchanting reminder of beach holidays.*

Shell mirror

A collection of shells are glued around the mirror's frame so that they overlap one another. White shells, plentiful on sea shores, are used to build up the frame's depth. The more unusual shells are placed prominently or picked out with paints in seaside shades of green, pale turquoise and coral.

You will need

◇ A mirror with a plain frame
◇ Shells
◇ Glue and bleach
◇ Watercolour paints
◇ Varnish

Making the shell frame

Boil the shells in a mixture of water and bleach for about an hour, then leave them to dry. Brush watercolour paint on to any interesting shell shapes which are worth drawing attention to. Then brush a thin coat of varnish over every shell.

After the varnish has thoroughly dried, glue the shells on to the frame. Begin with the more ordinary shells in your collection and take care to build up a reasonably even surface. Lastly, glue on the more interesting and colourful shells so that they stand out on the frame.

△ Just a few decorative shells can be used to create an unusual hair ornament. A simple method is to buy a cheap plastic slide (barrette) and glue the shells on to it.

▽ The joy of shellwork is that only a minimum of readily available materials are needed for you to create interesting and unusual pieces.

△ Shellwork transforms this ordinary chair. The shells are painted to pick up the colours of the sea shore. Bear in mind that, if shellwork is to be left outside, metallized car paints can give subtle, permanent colour.

Natural jewellery

*In autumn, trees and hedgerows provide a wealth of
exquisite natural materials. Make the most of an abundance of
these cheap resources by collecting acorns, pine
cones and seed pods, and use them to create beautiful and
unusual pieces of jewellery at very little cost.*

Autumn is the best season for gathering up all sorts of seeds, pods and nuts and using them to create your own attractive, unusual jewellery. Acorns, pine cones and various types of seed pods, once decorated with a hint of gold and varnished, can be transformed into beautiful necklaces, bracelets, earrings or brooches. Combine natural materials found in parks or woods with different types of beans and nuts which are available in shops.

The tones of natural leather blend well with pods, nuts and beans, making the ideal choice for the bands of necklaces and bracelets. Always use leather rather than suede as this can become greasy.

Preparing materials

If any of the natural materials you have selected are still green, ensure that you dry them completely before use by hanging them upside down in either a warm room or an airing cupboard. Keep only the perfect ones; if any item is brittle or rough to the touch do not use it.

Planning a design

Plan your design by arranging the seeds and pods on a sheet of paper. This gives a good idea of where to place each item. Once you have decided on a design, sketch it on to paper. Use it as a reference to show where each item will fit in and where the materials will be attached to the leather bands.

When choosing which materials to include in a piece of jewellery, it is best to use a limited variety of items as their repetition gives the design impact. A single item, unless large and prominently positioned just looks out of place if it is not balanced by a similar large item. Experiment with different combinations of materials before making your final choice.

◁ *In autumn, trees such as horse chestnuts and firs produce a variety of shapely and richly coloured nuts and cones. Collect them to make interesting jewellery to enhance clothes in natural colours such as ginger-brown, ochre and olive green.*

Pod necklace

1 Cut away the flower shapes on top of the poppy seed pods as they may damage your garments.

2 If you like, brush touches of gold paint on to the pods, seeds and beans to enliven them.

3 If pod, seed and cone segments are not completely dry before they are varnished, they may go mouldy. To prevent this, make sure they are as dry as possible and varnish them in two stages. Coat one side first, leave it to dry for six hours, then varnish the other side. This is also the easiest way to apply the varnish.

4 Make a sketch of the piece of jewellery, showing where the different materials are to be attached to the leather.

5 From the leather, cut two 12 x ⅜in (30 x 1cm) strips, for the neckband. From the remaining leather cut extra strips about ⅛in (3mm) wide and circles of leather about ¾in (2cm) in diameter. The extra strips and circles will be used to attach more pods and seeds along the neckband.

You will need

◇ Scrap of natural-coloured leather about 12 x 4in (30 x 10cm).
◇ Poppy seed pods
◇ Whole nutmegs
◇ Broad beans
◇ Large pine cone segments
◇ Eucalyptus pods
◇ Varnish

◇ Gold paint if desired
◇ Button or Velcro
◇ Paper clips
◇ Craft knife or sharp scissors
◇ Small pointed brush, about size number 5
◇ Solvent to clean paint from brush
◇ All-purpose clear adhesive

6 Cut each neckband lengthways into three ⅛in (3mm) wide strips, leaving ¾in (2cm) uncut at one end. Plait one neckband, starting at the uncut end, to a length of 10in (25cm). Place a clip — a paper clip will do — over the cut end to stop the plait unravelling. Repeat for the second band. The seeds and pods will be attached to the unplaited ends.

7 Using a strong cotton, tie the two bands together at the end of plaited sections and remove clips.

8 Trim the unplaited sections of strips to different lengths so that the pods and seeds will hang

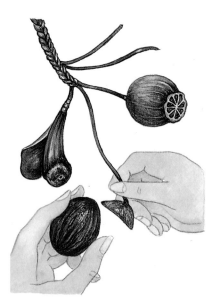

well. To make a mount to attach seeds, cut a hole in centre of each leather circle. Thread a strip of leather through hole and secure with glue. Apply glue to underside of circles, then wrap circle around top of the seed or pod. For flat seeds the circle may need to be cut and overlapped at the back.

9 Hide the join at base of plait with an extra pod. Secure with a strip of leather, wrapped around top of pod and the join. Glue strip at intervals while wrapping it.

10 Make extra mounts for more seeds and pods as described in step 8. Add items further up the necklace by looping strips through the plait. Adjust the length then glue seeds or pods to the mounts.

11 To make a fastening for the necklace, either cut a small slit on one end of the leather band and sew a suitable button on to the other side, or use Velcro.

▷ *Leaf-shaped silver earrings are decorated with varnished acorns. Glued neatly inside the curling leaves, the acorns make an eye-catching feature.*

Rolled beeswax candles

*Try nature's way of throwing light
on a special occasion by rolling your own pure beeswax candles.
Light the wick, take in the natural honey-like
fragrance and you will be able to enjoy the delights of
a traditional and practical craft.*

Beeswax is the oldest wax known and is still regarded as one of the finest fuels for candle making. Ever since their first appearance in Roman times, pure beeswax candles and have been seen as special.

Today, many people can afford to treat themselves to the luxury of these long-burning, naturally fragrant candles, and the most economical way is to use preformed beeswax sheets. These sheets, which are available from good craft shops, eliminate the need for using large amounts of molten wax. Leftover scraps from a beeswax sheet can be used to decorate the rolled up candle; and, if you want to make paraffin wax candles, scraps of beeswax can be added to improve the appearance and slow down the burning of these cheaper candles.

You will also need a wick: these are classified according to the finished diameter of the candle: a 1½in (37mm) wick will burn in a candle up to that diameter.

Rolling a candle

Follow these simple instructions for a candle that has the colour and texture of honeycomb. One sheet of beeswax, rolled as described below, will give you an 8in (20cm) candle, 1in (2.5cm) in diameter.

You will need
◇ 1 sheet of beeswax
◇ A length or ready-made 1½in (37mm) wick, available from craft shops
◇ Scissors

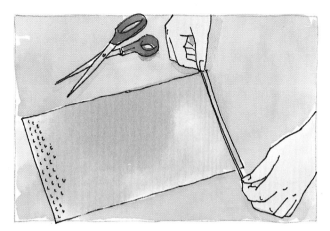

1 Working on a clean, flat surface, measure out a length of wick a few inches longer than the width (the shorter side) of the beeswax sheet.

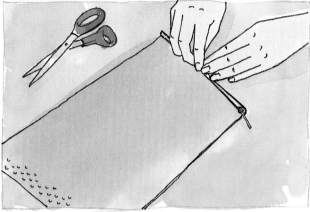

2 Pinch a corner of wax off the sheet and reserve for priming the wick. Secure the wick by turning over the edge of the wax sheet and pressing down.

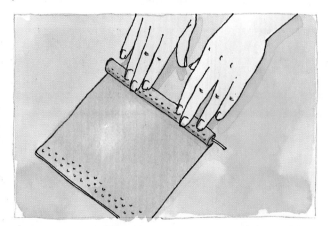

3 Roll the candle carefully, ensuring that the base is level. When fully rolled, press the outside edge against the candle to prevent it unrolling.

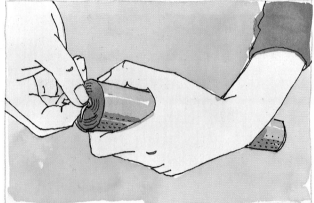

4 Trim the wick to about ½in (1.2cm). Pinch the small piece of reserved beeswax around the base of the wick so that it is primed and ready to light.

Variations on the basic candle can be made by cutting the sheet in half and rolling a shorter candle of double thickness. Alternatively, use two sheets for a long, thick candle or roll from the long edge of the sheet along the short edge for a long, slim candle.

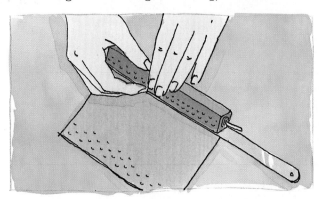

A square-shaped candle can be made by following the instructions for the basic candle, but using a ruler when rolling to help form the straight sides.

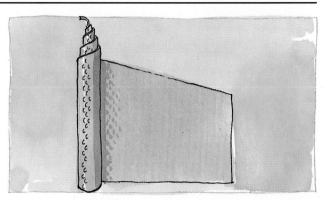

A tapered candle is made by altering the shape of the beeswax sheet before rolling. Use a knife and ruler to cut off a triangular section across one corner. Start rolling from the side opposite the shortened edge. If a large section is cut off, leaving one side much shorter than the other, the result will be an exaggerated spiral. For a gently pointed candle, cut away a small section, shortening one side only slightly.

Growing bulbs

*Flowering bulbs have always been popular
for indoor displays. Traditionally grown in soil, bulbs are ideal
candidates for hydroculture, or soilless planting.
Use a glass planter as it is just as fascinating to watch the
roots grow as it is to see the bulbs bloom.*

Bulbs are perfect plants for adding seasonal colour to your home. They are widely available and come in a wonderful range of blooms. Most bulbs can be successfully grown indoors without soil, using hydro-culture. Use special bulb jars, or grow in a mixture of gravel and pebbles, to support the bulbs above a water and plant food solution.

What are bulbs?
Technically, bulbs are storage or-gans, made of overlapping leaves that surround a young plant. The term 'bulb' also includes corms, which are thickened stem bases with papery coats (crocuses, for ex-ample); and tubers, which are thick-ened fleshy roots (such as gloxinia). All types of bulbs produce roots, leaves and flowers, and store food and water, for surviving dormancy or drought.

Buying bulbs
Bulbs are sold either in flower or in a dormant state. Dormant bulbs are cheaper, and you can enjoy watching them grow. Indoors, hardy bulbs, such as narcissi, provide a once-only display: they can't flower indoors again so once the blooms have died down they must be discarded or planted outdoors. Tender bulbs, such as cyclamen, can provide an an-nually recurring seasonal display.

Growing bulbs
Bulbs follow a basic cycle of growth, flowering and rest. Plant bulbs when dormant, water lightly to encourage growth, then feed and increase watering once growth starts. Most bulbs flower best in bright light.

Temperature needs vary: hardy bulbs like cool conditions, while forced bulbs need longer exposure to cold to start growing. Continue feeding until after flowering, then gradually stop to encourage dormancy.

Storage

Before storing bulbs, remove the old flower head. Leave the old leaves and stems attached to the bulb, as they help provide energy for future growth. Store bulbs when they are completely dry and re-plant them when the growing season starts. Some bulbs, such as cyclamen and tuberous-rooted begonias, are often discarded when in fact they can be left to grow year after year!

Hydroculture

Hydroculture provides a plant with everything it needs — nutrients, water, oxygen and anchorage — without using soil. It involves growing plants in containers filled with water and gravel, or pebbles, to which soluble plant foods are added. The plant's roots grow down through the layers of gravel to the water and fertilizer 'reservoir' at the bottom of the container.

Bulbs are ideal for growing by hydroculture, because they have their own, built-in supply of nutrients. As long as the bulb itself is kept fairly dry, to stop it rotting, its roots will grow in the waterlogged conditions. This is why bulbs can also be effectively grown in bulb jars; the roots feed in the water while the bulb remains dry.

Brightly coloured hyacinths and narcissi make interesting displays when grown using both bulb jars and the more involved hydroculture systems.

Grouping bulbs

Small bulbs look best grown *en masse*, several of one type per pot. Larger bulbs are often grown singly, but planting *en masse* can make a more impressive display, especially for tall-stemmed hippeastrums and lilies. The exact spacing between bulbs varies; those with upright growth are usually placed closer together than those with spreading leaves or flowers, while bulbs with wide-spreading leaves, such as cyclamen, look attractive grown singly.

For the best results, do not mix different types of bulbs or different coloured varieties. A mixed display may flower at different times, and so spoil the effect of the display. One exception may be mixing bulbs with the same flowering time and cultivation needs: a dish garden of snowdrops and crocuses, for example.

Suitable containers

Most bulbs flower best if pot-bound, so use containers 1½ times a bulb's diameter for single planting, or just large enough to hold groups, planted the correct distance apart. For a traditional display, plant with soil in heavy terracotta pots.

Hydroculture containers

Most bulbs can grow without soil in a container that does not have a drainage hole, filled with gravel and water. A clear glass container is ideal for showing the layers of gravel and stone chippings, as well as displaying root growth. It makes checking the water level easier, to avoid waterlogging. Other containers without drainage holes, such as wooden bowls, soup tureens and vases, are also suitable.

Special glass bulb vases designed to hold large bulbs, such as hyacinths, just above the water make an attractive alternative.

Hydropot narcissi

Plant bulbs in a decorative glass container prepared by building up alternating layers of gravel, stone chippings and charcoal. You could also add pebbles, grit, perlite or special expanded clay pellets to create decorative layers of different textures.

Materials and equipment

Container The container needs to be completely watertight, with a broad base to help keep it stable.

Natural stone chippings are ideal for lining the bottom of a container where the water reservoir is held. They are available in shades of cream, grey, brown or white and can look quite attractive.

Gravel is also used to build up the layers in the glass container, to create a more textured effect.

Charcoal is added to the water to keep it slightly acidic and, therefore, free from bacteria and algae. (Peat is sometimes used as an alternative to charcoal.)

Fertilizer Buy a special hydro-culture fertilizer, which is weaker than standard compost fertilizer. Or mix an ordinary liquid fertilizer with some water. Make sure that the solution is weaker than that used for plants grown in compost, as water-borne fertilizers will come into direct contact with the roots and could scorch them.

Bulbs Buy these in a dormant state.

You will need

◇ Glass container
◇ White stone chippings
◇ Charcoal
◇ Gravel
◇ Narcissus bulbs
◇ Black plastic bag
◇ String

▷ *A cluster of narcissus bulbs planted in a glass container provides an attractive and unusual indoor display. Create this decorative effect by building up layers of gravel, stone chippings and charcoal. The glass container enables you to see the fascinating patterns woven by the roots as they push down through the various layers towards the food and water solution.*

1 Wash the gravel and stone chippings. Line the bottom of the container with 1¼in (3cm) of stone chippings. Cover this with a layer of gravel and then a layer of charcoal pieces. Use the stone chippings to fill the container to about ¾ full. Then make shallow depressions for the bulbs.

2 Place each narcissus bulb in one of the depressions, leaving the tip of each one showing just above the surface, and a small gap between each bulb. Use stone chippings to fill any spaces around them. Add water to just below the level of the bulbs.

3 Cut a black plastic bag large enough to cover the container. Use string to secure the bag. Stand the container in a cool place. After about four weeks open the bag to check if the bulbs need more water. Do not allow all the water to evaporate.

4 Remove the bag after 8-10 weeks, when the roots have reached about ½in (12mm) in length. Place the container where it will get more warmth and light. Use stakes and plant ties to support the narcissi stems and leaves.

DESIGN IDEAS

△ For a bright indoor display, plant small groups of blue iris reticulata (miniature irises). You can either plant in attractive ceramic pots or, for a more unusual display, disguise the pots with a covering of twigs, tied together with raffia.

▽ Group dainty, lavender-coloured grape hyacinth bulbs together in a simple earthenware plant pot. Add a touch of rural sophistication to the display by scattering dried autumn leaves over the surface.

△ Display yellow iris reticulata in a canework basket, decorated with an assortment of pretty sea shells.

TIP	WATERING

If your area has hard water, boil it (and then allow to cool) before use. This helps to prevent mineral deposits, such as white limescale, from blocking the pores in the pellets, stopping them from drawing water from the reservoir.

Bottle gardens

*Bring a little corner of the great outdoors into
your home by creating your own bottle garden. It is surprisingly
simple to make and, with a little careful planning,
you will be rewarded with an attractive, long-lasting display that
needs the minimum of care and attention.*

If you live in a flat and are longing for a garden, or simply find that your favourite houseplants fail to thrive in your centrally heated home, a bottle garden might be just the thing to bring a little lushness into your life.

Apart from looking highly decorative, a bottle garden provides the extra humidity that many plants miss in today's modern homes. Smoky and dusty air is excluded from the plants so that leaf pores never get clogged, and they are protected from draughts and any sudden temperature changes.

Almost any type of large transparent container, including glass flagons, wine-making demi-johns, old-fashioned sweet jars or even a goldfish bowl, can be used to house your garden. You do not have to buy any special equipment as everything you need to plant your garden can be adapted from ordinary kitchen utensils.

You do need to know which plants to choose, how best to display them and have a moderately steady hand when planting them. The result of your efforts will be rewarded with a long-lasting, low-maintenance indoor garden.

Miniature trowel

Plant spray

Muslin

Paper chute

Charcoal

Peat

Pebbles

Sand

Loam-based compost

Materials and equipment

Selection of plants

Choose small, slow-growing plants of differing textures and shapes, which thrive in the same environment. Avoid flowering species as these have a limited season. Instead, introduce bright colours by including coloured leaved plants.

Whether you buy young plants from garden centres or nurseries, take cuttings from friends' houseplants or propagate your own seedlings, make sure that the roots are well established before planting.

Drainage material

This goes in the bottom of the container, so that the potting compost does not become waterlogged. Make this by mixing a handful of charcoal chips with clay aggregate pebbles or small washed stone pebbles. The charcoal prevents any standing water from turning sour. The drainage layer should be covered with a sheet of muslin or fine gauze to prevent compost from washing down into it and clogging the pores.

Compost mix

Make this by combining two parts compost potting soil (a mixture suitable for potting on established plants), two parts coarse sand and one part moss peat (peatmoss). This compost mix will ensure that the plants remain slow growing yet healthy.

Glass containers

Ideally the glass container should be non-coloured as this allows the maximum amount of sunlight to penetrate. Light green or pale brown tinted glass can also be used, but this type of container will restrict your choice of plants to shade-loving species.

To facilitate easy planting, make sure that the neck or opening of the container is a minimum of 2in (5cm) in diameter.

Homemade tools

Many containers have fairly narrow openings which call for long, thin-handled tools. Tape or wire a fork and spoon to lengths of garden cane for useful planting tools. Use a spool wedged on to a cane, to firm the compost around plants and lengths of cane for lowering plants in the compost. You will also need a sheet of stiff paper to make a chute (funnel) – this makes pouring pebbles, charcoal and compost into the container easier and less messy.

To care for your garden you will need a piece of sponge attached to cane for wiping away condensation and plant debris; a scalpel or razor blade, similarly attached, for tidying up dead leaves and a long piece of wire, looped at the end, for pulling out dead or overgrown plants and pruned plant material.

A plant spray and a winemaker's plastic funnel and tube are useful for occasional misting or watering.

Maidenhair fern

Ivy

Dumb cane

Variegated creeping fig

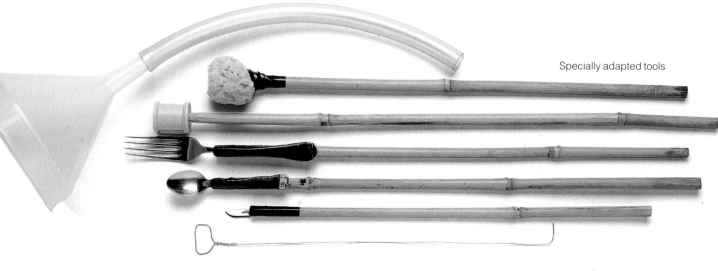

Plastic funnel and tube

Specially adapted tools

Recommended plants

Green foliage
Boston fern (*Nephrolepis exaltata bostoniensis*)
Button fern (*Pellaea rotundifolia*)
Creeping fig (*Ficus pumila minima*)
Ivy (*Hedera helix* dwarf varieties)
Lady fern (*Athyrium filix-femina* 'Minutissima')
Maidenhair fern (*Adiantum capillus-veneris*)
Maidenhair spleenwort (*Asplenium trichomanes*)
Mind-your-own-business (*Helxine/Soleirolia soleirolii*)
Moss fern (*Selaginella*)
Peacock plant (*Calathea makoyana*)
Peperomia bushy varieties
Polybody fern (*Polypodium vulgare*)

Coloured foliage
Aluminium plant (*Pilea cadierei*)
Arrowhead vine (*Syngonium podophyllum* varieties)
Caladium
Cretan brake fern (*Pteris cretica* 'Albolineata')
Croton (*Codiaeum variegatum pictum* narrow-leaved varieties)
Dumb cane (*Dieffenbachia maculata* varieties)
Earth stars (*Cryptanthus* species)
Goodluck plant (*Cordyline terminalis*)
Mosaic plant (*Fittonia argyroneura nana*)
Mother-of-thousands (*Saxifraga stolonifera* 'Tricolor')
Polka-dot plant (*Hypoestes phyllostachya*)
Prayer plant (*Maranta leuconeura*)
Ribbon plant (*Dracaena sanderana*)

Before you start
Select attractive plants in a range of sizes — taller ones for the back or centre, shorter ones for the front or edges — and plan the arrangement.

Before planting up, make sure that the container you are using is thoroughly clean and dry. As well as looking ugly, dirt deposits will stop sunlight penetrating through the glass and could also harbour troublesome fungal diseases.

Peperomia

Mind-your-own-business

Moss fern

Boston fern

Polka-dot plant

Planting up a bottle garden

△ *This attractive display is simple to make and easy to maintain.*

You don't need to be an experienced gardener, or indeed have green fingers, in order to create this simple yet effective display of indoor plants.

You will need
◇ A large glass bottle
◇ Plant selection
◇ Drainage material (pebbles and charcoal)
◇ Muslin or fine gauze
◇ Compost mix (potting soil)
◇ Miniature trowel or scoop
◇ Specially adapted tools
◇ Plant spray (mister)
◇ Plastic funnel and tube
◇ Pebbles, moss, pieces of bark or twigs for ground cover (optional)
◇ Paper chute (funnel)

1 Using a paper chute, pour a layer of drainage material on to the base of a clean, dry bottle. Cover with a layer of muslin or gauze, then add the compost mix.

2 Use a long-handled spoon to spread the compost and firm it gently. If you want a tiered display, bank up the compost towards the back of the container. Make the first planting hole.

3 Lower the first plant into its hole, using two canes or two long-handled spoons. Then fill in the hole. Repeat the procedure for the rest of the plants, leaving the central ones until last.

4 After planting plants or groups of plants, firm down the compost using a cotton-reel wedged on to the end of a bamboo cane. Make sure that none of the leaves is buried.

5 Bare patches can be filled with fresh moss, twigs, bark or pebbles. Use a wire hook to insert moss and a plastic tube or paper chute to scatter pebbles.

6 Spray the compost and foliage with tepid water. If the compost is very dry, use a plastic funnel and tube to water it. Clean sides of bottle with sponge.

◆ TIP	AFTERCARE

Place in a bright place near to a window but not in direct sunlight. You can tell the bottle has reached the right humidity level when there is just a trace of condensation on the glass. Remove any excess water with a sponge; add water if there is no condensation. When growing ferns and waxy-leaved plants, insert a stopper in the bottle to maximize humidity. Leave enough headroom for plants — leaves squashed against the side will rot.

CHAPTER II

FLORAL ARRANGEMENTS

◇

◇

Traditional flower arranging

*Carefully structured flower arrangements add
a formal touch to an important occasion and enhance traditional
decor. By choosing appropriate flowers and foliage
and following some simple rules for more stylized arrangements,
you can create your own stunning displays.*

Over the last century, professional flower arrangers have developed formal styles of display. The art of flower arrangement became popular in Edwardian England when seasonal garden flowers were massed in huge bouquets for en-hancing the home.

Many of the techniques used today use more limited amounts of flowers and foliage. Orderly, shaped arrangements bring extra impact to the display. By wiring the stems of some of the plants and leaves they can be positioned precisely so that the natural curve of a branch or the bend of a stem does not dictate the shape of the arrangement.

Proper preparation or condition-ing of flowers before they are arranged will ensure they last.

Tools and equipment
Containers
The container may form an impor-tant part of the display, or it may be completely masked by the flowers and foliage. The important point is to ensure that the con-tainer is stable — tall, shaped arrangements are surprisingly heavy. The proportions of con-tainers which are on show should also be considered, as the arrange-ment should look well-balanced. As a rough guide, the plant material should be arranged so that it is 1½ times the height and width of the container.

Ornamental supports
There are many ornamental sup-ports and accessories which have become popular as part of a floral display: art deco ladies, shallow open baskets, candlesticks and even pieces of driftwood. These will often dictate a shape for the dis-play: a leaping dolphin suggesting an arched arrangement or a paper fan suggesting a flat, crescent-shaped display.

Foam and wire
For most displays, the stems should be anchored in florist's foam. This in turn must be firmly anchored to the container. The florist's foam may be fitted on to prongs (some plastic flower containers have built-in prongs), stuck down with special clay or held in place with wire. In a narrow-necked container, the foam may be fitted snugly into the top and held with adhesive tape.

Florist's wires

To hold some plants erect and give others just the right curved shape, florist's wire can be used. For stems, heavy duty stub wires can be used, but you may also need finer wires to hold individual leaves in place. Any wire which shows should be bound with special tape known as gutta percha (floral tape), available from florist's suppliers.

You will also need good secateurs, a plant spray (mister) and an indoor watering can.

Choosing plant material

The shapes and colours of the flowers you choose will dictate the look of the final floral arrangement — whether you pick them from your garden or buy them. There are various elements to any arrangement — some stems will set the structural shape, prize specimens form a focal point and others fill out the display, adding colour and texture to the arrangement.

Types of flower shape

Columnar

Antirrhinum
Bells of Ireland
Delphinium
Eremurus
Eucomis
Foxglove
Gladiolus
Hyacinth
Liatris
Lupin
Red-hot poker
Stock

Rose (double)
Zinnia (double)

Ball

Agapanthus
Allium
Carnations and pinks
Chrysanthemum (double)
Mophead hydrangea
Nerine
Peony (double)
Ranunculus

Disc

Achillea
Candytuft
Cow parsley
Dill
Lacecap hydrangea
Sedum

Thistle-like

Knapweed
Echinops
Globe artichoke
Sea holly

Daisy-like

Aster
Calendula
Chrysanthemum (single)
Cosmos

Nerine

Carnation

Gypsophila

Michaelmas daisy

Hogweed

Marigold

Hyacinth

Dahlia (single)
Dimorphotheca
Doronicum
Fleabane
Gaillardia
Gerbera
Marguerite
Michaelmas daisy
Strawflower
Sunflower
Zinnia (single)

Lacey, feathery
Alchemilla
Astilbe
Gypsophila
Heuchera
Ornamental grasses
Sea lavender
Soapwort

Trumpet
Amaryllis
Clivia
Daffodil
Freesia

Hippeastrum
Lily
Montbretia
Narcissus

Sculptural/dramatic
Anthurium
Bird of paradise
Cockscomb
Iris
Orchid
Protea
Tulip

Cup
Anemone
Camellia (single)
Godetia
Hellebore
Peony (single)
Rose (single)
St John's wort

Pendant
Hazel
Love-lies-bleeding

Foliage for flower arranging
Asparagus fern
Bear grass
Beech
Berberis
Bergenia
Box
Butcher's broom
Cotoneaster
Cypress
Eucalyptus
Euonymus
False cypress
Galax
Hosta
Ivy
Laurel
Leather-leaf fern
Mexican orange
Pittosporum
Scottish broom
Smilax
Viburnum

Clivia

Rose

Iris

Tulip

Daffodil

Eucalyptus

Smilax

Freesia

Anemone

Conditioning plants

Give plants a good soak and prepare the stems. Trim the bottoms of soft stems on a slant and split about one inch from the bottom. Peel the bark from the base of woody stems and crush. Cut large hollow stems off flat.

Always remove any leaves which are below the water level, as they tend to turn water sour. The leaves of some plants should be stripped altogether or you will find that the leaves begin to turn yellow before the blooms fade. Leaves which should be stripped include lilac, statice and Peruvian lilies.

Wiring stems

When building up a display use the natural lines of the plants to dictate the shape of the arrangement. However, occasionally you will need to cheat and add wires to hold trails of ivy in gentle curves or support flower heads. Do this before you finish the arrangement — it is not a good idea to try to revive a drooping arrangement by adding wires later.

Hollow stems

Hollow stems can be strengthened with wires threaded up through the base of the plant. Push the wire up until the end comes through the centre of the head, then bend the end of the wire over to anchor it.

Leaves

1 To hold leaves at just the right angle, thread fine florist's wire through the centre of the leaf, piercing it on either side of the main vein.

2 Take the ends of the wire down the line of the stem and repeat for each leaf which needs control. Bind the stem with gutta percha to hide the wires.

Buds

1 To support sprays of buds and heavier buds such as roses, which are likely to bend, pierce the bud base with wire.

2 Wrap the wire around the stem, adding a sturdier stub wire to support floppy stems.

3 Cover the wire with tape, binding it around the stem, working from just under the head of the flower down the stem.

Planning

Once you have chosen a basic shape, establish the height of the display, using the tallest stem, or 'vertical'; then the width, using one or two stems, or 'laterals'. Work proceeds down and in from these extremities, with shorter stems - echoing the lines of the verticals and laterals.

The 'point of origin' is usually at the base of the vertical. This is the imaginary spot where all the stems should appear to meet, though they can not actually do so. The point of origin gives a sense of orderly movement to traditional displays.

The axis is the imaginary central line, often vertical, around which a display is built up. Keep it fixed in your mind as you work; symmetrical displays have about the same number of stems both sides of the axis, while asymmetrical displays have a different visual weight either side of the axis.

Finally, a focal point — the centre of interest — gives a sense of structure to the display. Often, the point of origin draws the eye. A flower or flower cluster noticeably larger than the rest also acts as a focal point, as does a concentration of flowers in bright colours.

Shapes and styles

The shape of an arrangement should depend on three things: the plant material you have available, the container and the setting it is to go in. There are traditional shapes for displays, which are always popular as they are balanced and lend themselves to the forms of plant material. A traditional arrangement has a well defined outline with flowers and foliage densely massed within the outline.

Triangles

These are symmetrical or asymmetrical, with equal or unequal sides. Depending on the container and site, they may be tall or long and low in profile.

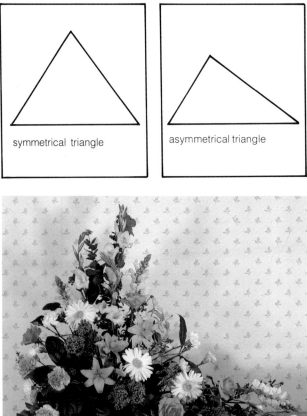

symmetrical triangle   asymmetrical triangle

Hogarth curves

These are shaped like a simplified letter S and the arrangement should be dense where the two curves meet, then taper towards the tips. It is only possible to create Hogarth curves in raised containers and wiring is often necessary. Hogarth curves are shown in greater detail over page.

L-shaped displays

A variation on the crescent, L-shaped designs are usually upright, with the vertical on the left. The display thickens where the two legs meet — an effect achieved by using shorter stems. The point of origin is often set to one side of the container, to help establish the asymmetry of the design.

L-shaped display

Vertical displays

Ovals and circles

These classic shapes lend themselves to more informal, massed displays. A simple and effective arrangement can be created by placing an even number of stems either side of a central stem. In raised containers, the whole outline of the display may be curved.

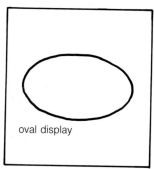

Horizontal displays

These should be handled with care, as they tend to be unstable. They defy the normal rules of proportion, having a sword-shaped outline, at least 1½ times the height of the container but no wider than it. Little material is needed to create a dramatic show. Vertical designs often have a modern feel and are ideal for making a display in a limited space.

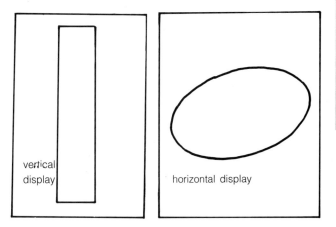

These are popular on dining tables as they do not interrupt the view across the table. Two horizontal stems set the length of the display and shorter central or asymmetric stems set the height. Flowers are added to flow from the vertical outwards.

A Hogarth curve arrangement

The elongated 'S' shape of the Hogarth curve makes an elegant and unusual display. When you are arranging the stems, use the way each naturally inclines and ensure that flowerheads do not all face in the same direction. Also place a fair amount of stems towards the back of the vase as this gives the arrangement a sense of depth.

You will need
◇ Raised china vase
◇ Roses
◇ Rhododendrons
◇ Weigela
◇ Florist's foam block
◇ Florist's wire
◇ Sticky tape
◇ Scissors

1 Place a florist's foam block in a raised vase, using tape to hold it firmly in place.

2 Use about five of the tallest stems to create the basic outline of the arrangement, supporting them with wire if necessary.

3 Gradually add flowers and foliage to enhance the flowing curves of the 'S' shaped design.

Hogarth curve

Japanese flower arranging

Japanese flower arranging or Ikebana is both artistic and full of symbolism. You do not have to be a dedicated follower to appreciate its simplicity, clarity of line and sheer elegance — and on a far more practical level, you can achieve impressive results on a shoestring budget.

The custom of using arrangements of flowers as ritualized temple offerings originated in Buddhist China. It was introduced to Japan in the sixth century AD, where it evolved into an elaborate art form known as Ikebana.

Today, the spiritual symbolism of Ikebana — which freely translated means 'keeping plants alive in containers filled with water' — can be a lifetime's study. You can, however, approach it in a relaxed way — as inspiration for understated flower displays.

Ikebana is practical and beautiful (as well as meaningful to its followers). Cut flowers and branches last longer displayed in the Eastern manner than in dense masses; Japanese flower arranging is far more economical, as with just a little material, you can create an infinite variety of designs.

Styles of Ikebana

The three main categories of Ikebana are the formal and classical *rikka*, which is usually seen only in temples, the relaxed *nageire* and *moribana*, which is arranged in a shallow dish. Each category has it own styles and variations and various Ikebana schools have their own interpretations. However, in all styles, asymmetry is the key. The 'springing point', where branches or stems enter the water, helps to create this deliberate lack of balance; a branch is never flanked either side with flowers for the same reason.

Principles of Ikebana

Most displays are based on three imaginary lines. The tallest (or principal) line symbolizes heaven and is often shaped like an archer's bow. The secondary line symbolizes humanity, it is roughly three-quarters the length of the primary line, when fully extended. The shortest line represents the earth and is a quarter of the principal line's length.

The principal line is usually one and a half to two times the height of a tall container plus the diameter, or one and a half to two times the width of a shallow container plus the depth. These lines are set at particular angles, depending on the style of Ikebana. The angles vary greatly and can even be horizontal.

Ikebana is three dimensional, with the angles set so that the branches lean forward and incorporate the spaces which form an important part of the design.

Materials and equipment
Flowers, foliage and branches

To the devotee, every plant is symbolic: pine means everlasting life; bamboo, resilience; early-flowering plum, courage, and so on. You can also select material by eye alone, choosing from seasonal, easy-to-come-by plants and flowers, but certain trees, shrubs and herbaceous flowers are traditional.

Any plants with the specific names *orientalis*, *japonica* or *sinensis*, meaning 'oriental', 'Japanese'

TIP	RULES OF IKEBANA

◇ The form and angle of the stems and branches is more important than that of the flowers and foliage.
◇ The stems and branches should not fill the mouth of the container. They should look stable and as if growing naturally from the same point on the surface of the water, which symbolizes soil.
◇ Use seasonal, easily obtained material rather than expensive or exotic flowers.
◇ The design should be balanced according to its position in the room, sweeping across a shelf, upright in an alcove or growing around a picture, for example.

and 'Chinese' are safe; shaped roots and driftwood can also be used.

Containers

Traditional containers can be any shape or size. Bear in mind that the size of the container dictates the size of the arrangement.

They can be free standing, wall hung or hanging; and ceramic, brass, iron, bronze, or bamboo, laquered wood or basketwork with a waterproof liner. Colours range from black to white, and bright hues to earthy, subtle shades. Avoid elaborate containers which

Traditional material

Trees and shrubs

Cultivated or wild cherry, pear, quince, plum, peach, almond or crab apple blossom; camellia, maple, chaenomeles, wintersweet, blackthorn, laburnum, tree paeony, bramble, pine, willow, dogwood, magnolia, yew, viburnum, spruce, broom, berberis, azalea, rhododendron, wisteria, honeysuckle and clematis.

Flowers and foliage

Iris, chrysanthemum, lily, aster, narcissi, bulrush, arum lily, marsh marigold and water lily, hosta, palm, reed, bamboo, begonia and iris foliage.

may distract from the display.

Oriental shops sell inexpensive containers, but you can improvise with a simple vase or dish.

Supports and tools

Pinholders (prongs) are used to support the material in wide, shallow displays. In tall vases, heavy metal coils or supports cut from branches are used. Try to get special, heavy Japanese pinholders, known as *kenzam*.

You will also need secateurs: purists use Japanese florist's scissors, known as *hasami*.

Positioning branches

1 Using a pair of secateurs or Japanese florist's scissors, cut diagonally across the end of each branch — shown here is pussy willow.

2 Secure the branch on to the pinholder by pushing it down firmly in an upright position, with the slanted end facing inwards.

3 Position the branch by bending it to the desired angle, away from the slanted edge, so that the sharp prongs of the pinholder grip the bark firmly.

Moribana style Ikebana

In this style of Ikebana a pinholder helps achieve precise positioning. The materials required are shown overleaf.

1 Place a metal pinholder to the left of centre and to the front of a shallow, round, square or shell-shaped container.

2 Cut a branch of pussy willow to the desired length (twice the width plus the depth of the container). Place it in the pinholder, and angle it to the left so that it curves concavely away from the centre and leans forwards.

3 Take the second branch of pussy willow and cut it so that it is roughly ¾ the length of the principal branch. Insert it in the front left of the pinholder, repeating the curves of the principal line.

6 Inspect the display, removing any excess twigs or leaves that spoil the lines, using a sharp secateurs or *hasami*, Japanese florist's scissors. Make sure the dish is clean and debris free, place it in the position it is to occupy, then fill with water.

You will need
◇ Two branches of pussy willow
◇ Five Dutch irises
◇ Three soleil d'or narcissi
◇ Viburnum and juniper leaves as filler
◇ Shallow container
◇ Metal pinholder (Japanese style *kenzam*, if possible)
◇ Secateurs or Japanese florist's scissors (*hasami*)

4 For the third line, take a long iris that is still in bud. Insert it in the front right of the pinholder so that it curves concavely to the right and leans forwards.

5 Add 'supporting' flowers. Insert two open irises and two soleil d'or to support the third line, and one iris and one soleil d'or slightly in front of the principal line. The slant of the supporting flowers should echo that of the line they are supporting. Add viburnum and juniper to mask the pinholder. The pinholder will be more effectively hidden if the foliage leans forwards.

Shallow container

Pussy willow

Metal pin holder

Japanese florist's scissors

Dutch irises

Soleil d'or narcissi

Viburnum

Juniper leaves

Flowers for weddings

*Floral displays are one of the most memorable
sights at a wedding and those carried by the bride and bridesmaids
will be photographed and remembered for years
to come. Learn how to wire and arrange bouquets and hoops
and save on florists' fees.*

Bridal bouquets, corsages, posies and hoops of flowers are timeless accessories at any wedding. They add a special finishing touch to the outfits worn by the bride and her attendants on this important day. Professional florists charge a great deal to make bridal bouquets and garlands but they can be successfully made at home for a fraction of the cost.

Most charming of all are garlands — circlets of flowers for the hair and the matching hoops designed for children to carry. These delightful arrangements bring an Edwardian touch to the bride's smallest attendants and they also look effective displayed in the church and at the reception. Hang hoops and circlets to decorate the reception hall or use circlets of flowers as the centrepiece for the tables at the reception.

This section shows which flowers to use for wedding displays, the type of equipment needed and how to wire flowers to make the garlands. You will find how to make a trailing bridal bouquet and a matching corsage on pages 45-48.

Styles and effects

White and pastel coloured flowers are the most popular choice for summer weddings. Choose a colour theme to run through all the flowers on display — at the church or register office and reception as well as those worn and carried by the bride and her entourage.

Over the last few years, it has become more and more popular to give small bridesmaids hoops of flowers to carry, often repeating the theme with circlets of flowers in their hair. These are not as stiffly wired as the bouquet and the corsage as they should have a more natural effect. However it is vital that they are firmly fixed to withstand the treatment they are likely to get from small children. Hoops and circlets are often decorated with ribbons and bows for extra colour.

Choosing flowers and foliage

Apart from considering the colour you want to use, it is important to choose flowers which will last for several hours out of water. As a general rule, the more waxy the texture of the petals, the better they will last. Orchids and lilies, for example, will last better than stocks or campanulas. Flowers in bud will last longer than those which are fully open.

The size and shape of the blooms is also going to contribute to the overall effect: if in doubt, go for classic combinations of ever-popular flowers — they have become classics because they work. Rosebuds, carnations and softer sprays of gypsophila are always a success. Look out, too, for composite flower heads, which can be divided into individual florets to make them go further: Peruvian lilies and Singapore orchids are suitable for more formal displays, while sweet peas and hydrangeas bring fresh, clear colours, reminiscent of English cottage gardens, to a display. Of course, flowers which are in season will be the most economical choice — you may even be able to use flowers from your own or friends' gardens.

A good range of foliage is also important in providing a backdrop for the flowers: choose small, neatly shaped leaves in tones to suit the colour scheme. Variegated leaves give a less heavy effect than solid, dark colours. Ivy is an excellent choice, adding trailing shapes to the arrangement, and variegated euonymus or mock orange also have suitably sized leaves. For bluer tones, choose eucalyptus, feathery blue rue or shrubby miniature hebe. And yet another delightful touch is to use sprigs of herbs such as rosemary, lavender or sage to bring soft colour and scent to the display.

Materials and equipment

Wire is used to hold individual flower heads and leaves in place. It is usually sold in convenient lengths, known as stubs. Get a good selection of different weights of wire, and always use the finest you can, to provide support without adding unnecessary bulk and weight.

Self-adhesive tape is used to cover the wire and re-create the stems of the plant material. Several different types are available:

Variegated ivy

Gypsophila

Freesia

Alstromeria lily

Rose

Eucalyptus

traditional gutta percha (floral tape) is made from natural gum, but you may find the various different coloured florists' tapes more convenient.

A plant spray (mister) is needed to keep the work fresh and cool.

Ribbon is often added to bouquets and other arrangements. Florists' ribbon is economical, but for such special occasion flowers, woven ribbon is usually a better choice. You may need to stitch individual bows in place or fix them with clear fabric adhesive.

You will also need other flower arranging equipment, such as sharp secateurs. An old block of florists' foam (oasis) is useful for holding wired sprays before you make up the arrangement, and a cardboard box is useful for holding and protecting the flowers once they are ready.

Conditioning

It is rarely possible to pick and arrange all the flowers for a wedding on the morning of the big day. But all the plant material should be as fresh as possible. As soon as you have picked or bought it, trim the ends of the stems and plunge them into a deep bucket of water (see pages 29-32). Leave them in a cool place until ready to use.

Once arranged, the displays should be sprayed and can be kept fresh overnight in a fridge. Put them in an open carboard box and slip them into a plastic bag, but make sure the bag does not touch any delicate petals.

Wiring flowers

Wiring may seem to be an artificial way to treat flowers, but with some styles and shapes it is the only way to ensure the flowers will hold their shape once the arrangement is finished. This particularly applies when making a large trailing bouquet (see page 45). The art of the florist is to make the arrangement appear natural by imitating the habit of the plants.

Wiring will also help the plant material to go further, as you will be able to make use of almost every leaf and floret. Large and unwieldy shapes like florists' carnations can be divided and re-arranged to suit the shape of the display. This is described on page 47

Preparation

Before you start to arrange the flowers estimate the number of individual flowers and sprays you will need, then wire and bind them. Wire the individual flower heads (see page 32). Divide and wire any florets and petals. Bind the wires and stems as you make up the display.

Wiring groups of flowers

The arrangements in this project have small clusters of flowers and foliage wired together, as well as individual flowers that have been wired as described in preparation.

△ *Group three to four flowers or stems of foliage together. Twist 12 gauge wire securely around the stems as shown. Cover the wire with florists' tape.*

Flower hoops

Hoops and circlets must be bound and taped to a firm base which will stand up to a little rough handling by the youngest bridesmaids. Hoops to be carried can be built up on toy hoops and covered with ribbon. Use the traditional hoops made of wood, if you can find them, or plastic toy hoops.

You will need
◇ A toy hoop
◇ Florists' wire guage 12
◇ Florists' tape
◇ Ribbon to bind hoop
◇ Silver reel wire
◇ Freesias
◇ Gypsophila
◇ 'Pale' pink roses
◇ Champagne pink roses
◇ Eucalyptus
◇ Variegated ivy
◇ Ivy

▷ *To achieve the best effect all the floral arrangements to be carried by the wedding party should co-ordinate. But it is important to choose blooms that suit the scale of the finished arrangement. The flowers used here to make the circlet for the young bridesmaid's hair are smaller and daintier than those used for the hoop.*

1 Bind the hoop with ribbon and secure with clear sticky tape neatly at the join. Twist ivy around the hoop and secure with 12 guage wire at intervals.

2 Wire individual flowers as described in 'Preparation'. Wire small clusters of flowers as shown in 'Wiring groups of flowers'. The small clusters should include groups of the same flowers as well as groups of foliage with flowers.

3 Arrange the wired flowers and foliage into two sprays, with a long trail of ivy towards the back of the spray. Before the spray is put onto the hoop, wire the single flowers and clusters into more manageable groups.

4 Position the two sprays together so that the wired ends overlap. Wire them together at the centre.

5 Position the spray on to the hoop, so that it covers the taped join. Wire it in place using silver reel wire that has been covered in tape. Twist the trails of ivy around the hoop and secure with wire

6 Disguise any wire that may show with extra trails of ivy.

Circlets

Circlets for the hair can be formed from the wired stems of the plants, bound tightly into a circle. However it is easier to make a wiring of the required size first, then tape the flower stems to the ring. The stems can be covered with ribbon if desired: choose a harmonious colour.

Secure the circlet to the head with long hairpins or stitch a hairgrip to the back of the circlet. Alternatively stitch ribbon or elastic to the hoop, and hide it under the hair.

You will need
◇ Milliners' wire
◇ 12 guage florists' wire
◇ Florists' tape
◇ Variegated ivy
◇ Freesias
◇ 'Pale' pink rosebuds
◇ Champagne rosebuds
◇ Gypsophila
◇ Eucalyptus
◇ Peruvian lilies

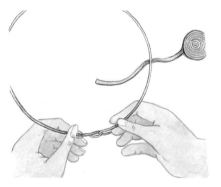

1 Measure the head of the person who is going to wear the circlet and cut a piece of milliners' wire slightly longer than this. Curve the wire into a hoop the correct size and twist the ends together. Make sure the ends lie safely. Cover hoop with tape.

◁ *A circlet of flowers is a perfect head dress for small bridesmaids.*

2 Wire small bunches of flowers and bunches of foliage together as shown on the previous page to make the hoop. The bunches can have much smaller stems. Cover the stems with florists' wire.

3 Wire and tape the bunches of flowers and foliage around the hoop, alternating the foliage with the flowers.

◆ TIP	HOLD STEADY

While you are working on an arrangement, stick all the pre-wired flowers and foliage into a block of Oasis so that it is ready to hand when you need it.

Trailing bouquet

Bridal bouquets and bridesmaids' flowers must be easy and comfortable to carry, hold their shape and be able to last out the big day. They can be shaped in a number of ways: simple posies, large sprays, even a single, perfect lily.

A formal, trailing bouquet is one of the best choices to complement a traditional wedding dress. This style of bouquet has a central focus of flower heads, surrounded by flowing buds and foliage. These are usually wired, to ensure that they hold their shape and to make best use of leaflets and flower heads. The stems or wires are also taped tightly in place, with the ends taken to a long point behind the centre of the bouquet, to give a firm 'handle' for the bride to grip without difficulty.

The bouquet shown here is made from readily available flowers and even though it is wired, it has a lovely natural look. Use the flowers shown here or substitute your own choice of blooms to co-ordinate with your wedding theme.

You will need
◇ 12 gauge florists' wire
◇ Florists' tape
◇ White freesias
◇ Alstroemeria lily
◇ Gypsophila
◇ Variegated ivy
◇ Eucalyptus
◇ Pale pink roses
◇ Champagne roses
◇ Silver reel wire
◇ Wide florists' ribbon

The arrangement
This bouquet has been built up from two sections, a wedge shaped bunch and a circular posy, to form the distinctive 'trailing' shape. The bouquet is held at the top by the stem wires, which are bent to form a handle, then decorated with ribbon. The flowers and foliage are wired before the bouquet is made and it is a good idea to wire the flowers into manageable bunches at stages as you work.

Preparation

1 Wire the roses on 12" lengths of 12 gauge wire and cover the stems and wire in florists' tape, (see pages 30-32). Wire the ivy in the same way.

2 Wire the freesias in clusters and cover the stems and wire in florists' tape. Repeat to make clusters of alstroemeria lilies and clusters of gypsophila. This method also makes the bouquet stable.

△ This trailing bouquet has an enchanting mixture of spring flowers to brighten a traditional wedding dress. And the bouquet is made at a fraction of the cost of buying one from a florist.

To make the bouquet

1 Select ¾ of the ivy stems for the trail. Stagger the different flowers through the ivy to form a wedge-shaped bunch about 8" (20cm) wide and 14" (35cm) long. As you work, wire the individual flowers and clusters into more manageable bunches using silver reel wire and tape.

2 For the top of the bouquet loosely group the flowers and foliage into a circular posy.

3 Position the trail into the centre of the posy and bend the wire of the trail at a 45° angle to the posy. Wire the trail into position.

4 Fill in the bouquet with the remaining flowers and foliage placing some in deep.

5 Trim the wires to a length that makes a comfortable handle for a bouquet. Make sure the handle is wired securely then tape it. Make sure that any sharp ends are covered.

6 Wrap florists' ribbon around the handle and tie in a firm double bow.

Corsage

It is customary for close family members of the bridal party to wear a corsage — a simple cluster of flowers and buds pinned to the lapel of a blouse or suit. The flowers used in the corsage should relate to the ones carried by the main wedding party. The corsage should also be wired and taped so that it will hold its shape throughout the day.

This corsage has been made from an exquisite combination of white freesias, variegated ivy and eucalyptus leaves.

△ *Freesias, combined with eucalyptus leaves and variegated ivy, make a charming corsage.*

You will need
◇ Florists' wire
◇ Florists' tape
◇ White ribbon
◇ A strong pin
◇ White freesias
◇ Variegated ivy
◇ Eucalyptus leaves

1 Wire and tape the flowers and foliage (see page 32).

2 Arrange a selection of blooms and foliage into an appealing display. The corsage should be a rectangular shape and not too large.

3 Wire the corsage together and cover the join with tape. Attach to the lapel with the pin.

TIP   **CONDITIONING**

Remember to keep the bouquet and corsage in top condition by following the guidelines given on page 32.

Carnations

Carnations are an ideal flower for weddings as they last particularly well. They are also sold in abundance during spring and summer — making them quite affordable. Both single and spray types come in a wide range of colours including peach, pink, creamy yellow and white hues, which all complement a wedding theme. Carnations can also be made to 'go further' by using the feathering technique.

Feathering carnations

Feathering is a useful technique for using the heavy heads of carnations in smaller, lighter arrangements. The technique can be used to create trailing 'buds' to match the larger flower heads. It involves separating the petals and regrouping them into smaller clusters, then wiring them.

1 Gently peel back the sepals at the base of the flower and pluck out individual petals.

2 Use a very fine wire to bind two or three petals together to make an appropriately sized floret.

3 Cover the wire with florists' tape to re-create the sepals and form a stem.

Separating florets

1 Cut individual flower heads from the main stem, leaving it about 1in (2.5cm) long. Pierce the base of the florets, twist the wire together and cover in tape.

2 Build up the separate florets into a natural-looking but more tightly grouped spray.

Sprays of ivy

1 Clip off the individual leaflets from the stem. Use a fine wire to pierce the leaves on either side of the main vein, bring the ends of the wire together at the base.

2 Bind the wire with florists' tape, adding further leaves down the length of the wire stem.

Making a buttonhole

A buttonhole is simple to make and gives a festive look to the attire of the groom, the father of the bride and the best man.

1 Cut a circular piece of card smaller than the flower head. Pierce the centre and make small cuts from the centre about ⅛in (3mm) long.

2 Carefully peel off the outer leaves and seed pod of the carnation. Push the circle of card up the stem to just below the flower head. Push wire through the back of the carnation. Wire a leaf – an ivy leaf for example (see page 32).

3 Bind the carnation and leaf together with florists' tape to complete the buttonhole. It will sit comfortably in position and add a touch of sophistication to a man's or woman's suit.

DESIGN LIBRARY

△ *A bridesmaid's coronet is made up of apricot roses and gypsophila set against a foil of ivy leaves.*

△ *An unbound wooden hoop is sparingly decorated with lilac bows and a selection of flowers including hydrangea, lesser periwinkle and veronica. The effect is pleasingly simple.*

▷ *A garland of delicate flowers — alstroemeria, antirrhinum and gypsophila — is twisted around a hoop entwined with pale grey ribbon. A large ribbon bow at the top of the hoop is the ideal finishing touch.*

Table centrepieces

*Make a happy break with tradition that will leave your
dining table looking welcoming. Using a wide range of inexpensive
materials, combined with interesting items collected
from the garden, you can create an attractive table decoration
for a fraction of the price of fresh flowers.*

50

New-look decoration

Dining tables tend to take up a lot of space and come alive only when they are properly dressed for dinner; the rest of the time they often appear dormant and dull. Traditionally, the solution to this probem has been to liven up this 'dead' area with a central display of flowers or fresh fruit. But these, too, have their problems — flowers wilt quickly and are expensive to replace; and a delicious display of fresh fruit is liable to disappear within days.

There is, however, an alternative which is both attractive and economical. Look around you — in your kitchen, around the house and in your garden — there are numerous things you can use to make unusual and exciting table decorations.

▷ *Brightly coloured or interestingly shaped root vegetables and gourds, ivy leaves, pebbles, bark, grasses, acorns, conkers, evergreen leaves and cones can all look as attractive as fresh flowers and have the added advantage of being longer lasting. Combine with candles and candlesticks, or even plastic fruit, for a centrepiece to suit all occasions. This cheery and colourful display will brighten up a bare table, while an elegant combination of ivy and a plain white candle would suit a more formal dinner party.*

Harvest displays

*Celebrate the harvest festival with bunches
of golden country grains and grasses, available in abundance
in late summer. A simple wheatsheaf, for
example, tied with a raffia plait, looks equally effective in
a church or at a special autumn party.*

Traditionally, autumn celebrations such as harvest festival marked the end of the bountiful summer growing season. Homes and village churches were bedecked with fresh garden produce, golden wheatsheaves and swags and garlands woven with dried grasses and cereals. These symbolic harvest displays make lovely decorations for the home during autumn, when home-grown flowers are in short supply.

Decorative uses

Grasses and cereals are versatile and relatively low-cost materials which can be tied into sheaves or arranged in baskets and containers to make impressive displays with a rustic feel. They can be combined with more costly dried plant materials, such as rose buds and lavender; their neutral colours balance and complement the rich hues of late summer fruits and flowers.

Church displays

In autumn, country churches are traditionally decorated with sheaves of wheat and baskets of garden produce to celebrate the harvest festival. The pew ends, church font and the base of the pulpit are all ideal places for special displays. Small sheaves made from wheat and barley can be grouped on the windowsills alongside jars of summer preserves, bread plaits and baskets of fresh garden produce. Always remember to ask permission before arranging displays in a church.

▽ *Celebrate the harvest season with a small sheaf of wheat tied up with a plait and hung on your door.*

Displays for the home

Stand a wheatsheaf in an unused fireplace, on the corner of a farmhouse-style dresser, in an alcove or on the corner of a kitchen work surface. Fill a container with one variety or a mixture of grasses, or make a flat design to hang on the wall. Add a few fresh or dried flowers for colour and contrast.

Another bygone autumn custom involved fixing dried grasses and flowers over the house front door to ward off evil spirits. Nowadays, door decorations, such as small sheaves or wreaths, can be used to welcome guests to a party.

Choosing grasses

Many different types of cereal, ornamental and wild grasses can be used in harvest displays. Cereal grasses, such as wheat, oats, barley and rye, provide subtle colour and texture. Ornamental grasses, such as golden foxtail, quaking grass and switch, also work well visually.

Obtaining cereal grains

If you live in the countryside it may be possible to gather a few cultivated grasses growing wild under hedges or by the wayside, where the seed has been scattered by birds or carried on the wind.

Bunches of dried grasses are also available from some florists and dried flower shops. Alternatively, grow your own cereals and ornamental grasses from seed.

Picking and drying

Grasses and cereals should be picked on a dry day when they are just turning golden; this must be done before the damp weather sets in and discolours them. To prevent damage, use a sharp knife or a pair of secateurs to cut the grasses.

To dry the cut grasses, either lie them out on a sheet of absorbent paper, stand them upright in a dry container or hang them upside down in a bunch. Leave them in a cool, dry room away from direct sunlight until they have dried.

Containers

For the best effect, choose a container with straight sides and a wide neck: it should be half the height of the grasses at most. This enables the firm, straight stems to stand tall and stately while the seed heads fan out over the rim of the container. If the container is too deep it will restrict the natural movement of the stems.

To enhance the rustic look of the grasses, display them in a country-style container, such as a wicker basket, a terracotta vase, or even a hollowed-out piece of wood.

Raffia

Raffia is available from craft stores and some florists. It is a cheap and useful material for flower arranging. It can be tied or plaited to form the base of wreaths, garlands and swags; alternatively, it can be used as a decoration to add interest to plain containers.

▷ *A trio of wheat sheaves adds an air of harvest plenty, displayed on an old dresser with favourite pieces of colourful pottery.*

Making a harvest sheaf

A harvest sheaf is very easy to make using a wide selection of dried grasses — wheat or black-eared barley look especially effective. Here we have used black-eared barley. Whichever type of grass is used, the stems should be tightly bunched together to make a lush and abundant harvest display.

You will need
◇ Raffia, made into a plait
◇ A generous bunch of black-eared barley
◇ String or fine gauge stub wire

▽ *Feathery tops give a sheaf of black-eared barley a soft outline.*

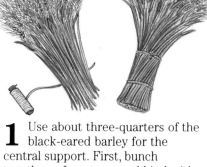

1 Use about three-quarters of the black-eared barley for the central support. First, bunch together a few stems and bind with string or wire. Gradually build up the support in layers, binding each layer with string or wire.

2 Using the remaining stems, form a neat outer layer around the central support. Use string or wire to bind the stems at a point about halfway along the stems so that they splay out in a spiral.

3 Making sure the heads of the wheat are in place, carefully trim stem ends to an equal length.

4 Tie the raffia plait around the sheaf to cover the binding and to form an added decoration.

Flat-topped display

A flat-topped basket arrangement makes an attractive alternative to a wheatsheaf and looks equally effective displayed in a church or on a side-table in the sitting room.

You will need
◇ Dry florists' foam
◇ Shallow basket
◇ Wheat
◇ A sharp knife
◇ Pair of scissors

1 Using a sharp knife, cut the foam to fit tightly into the base of the basket.

2 Make five bunches of wheat, each containing 30 stems. Trim evenly so that you have one bunch in each of the following lengths: 12in (30cm), 10in (25cm), 8in (20cm), 6in (15cm) and 4in (10cm).

3 Push the longest bunch of stems vertically into the centre of the foam block in the base of the basket. Add the rest of the wheat in bunches of 30 (refer to photograph for positioning).

4 Cut more stems of wheat to about 2in (5cm) long and use to fill around edge of basket.

5 For added impact, trim the seed heads with scissors to give a very flat surface.

◇ **TIP**   **SPRAYING GRASSES**

Spray cereals and grasses with ordinary hair lacquer to help prevent the stems wilting and the seeds falling off. This can be done either before or after the grasses have been dried.

△ *For a solid display, fill a basket or an old trug with flat-topped bunches of wheat. Cut the wheat to different lengths to add interest to the outline.*

▽ *Gentle natural light, softened by a stained glass window, enhances the golds, yellows and greens in this lovely arrangement of flowers and wheat.*

A festive wreath

*Welcome Christmas visitors by hanging a festive
wreath, made from lush foliage and seasonal fruits and nuts,
on a front door or in a hallway. As fresh flowers
are scarce, winter is the time to experiment with different
materials, to create an original design.*

Since early times, wreaths have been used as decorations. They are traditionally regarded as tokens of renewal, peace and friendship, so a festive wreath will ensure a special, warm welcome for visitors.

Texture and colour

By experimenting with an assortment of dried materials you can create a variety of textures, adding depth and appeal to a wreath. This may take a little more thought, but the effects can look lush and striking. For example, moss adds a velvety texture, while pine cones, nuts and bark give more of a rustic effect.

Use colour to help create a scheme; for example, red and green are traditionally winter colours, while pastel shades look wonderful in summer arrangements.

To make the wreath

1 Roll out a handful of damp sphagnum moss to form a fat sausage-shape that just fits around the circumference of the wire frame. Tie one end of the mossing wire to the frame. Keeping the moss tightly packed to an equal thickness all round, wind the wire tightly around the frame at ½in (1.2cm) intervals. Use scissors to trim off any straggling bits of moss.

A Christmas wreath
You will need
◇ 18in wreath frame
◇ A pair of scissors
◇ 12in stub (stem) wires
◇ 7in stub (stem) wires
◇ Reel of mossing wire
◇ 1yd (91cm) of ribbon
◇ Green gutta tape (floral tape)
◇ Holly, ivy, spruce
◇ Firm red and green apples
◇ Limes
◇ Walnuts
◇ Cinnamon sticks

4 Using this method, decorate the entire wreath with the bunches of foliage, leaving a 2in (5cm) gap between each set of leaves. Make sure that all the leaves are lying flat and facing the same way.

5 Thread a 12in (30cm) stub wire around the bottom of each fir cone, and twist the two ends together to form a stalk. Push the wire through the moss, bending it under to anchor the cones securely. For walnuts, push a 7in (18cm) stub wire through the base of the shell, and twist the two ends of wire together. (If necessary, use a blob of glue to stick one end of the wire to the shell.) Attach to the wreath by pushing the wire through the base.

Scent

Consider the appeal of fragrance when making a wreath, so choose materials that will give an appealing scent as well as look attractive. Evergreen leaves, such as pine, give off a musky, herbal aroma. And citrus fruits have a tangy sweetness, especially when mixed with the fragrance of star-anise and cinnamon sticks.

Materials and equipment

Wire frame to wire your materials to (available from your local florist or garden centre).
Sphagnum moss provides an ideal base.
Foliage is used to cover the moss base. Use spruce, ivy and holly to create a traditional winter wreath, while corn and barley look splendid in summer.

Fruit should be firm and healthy, with strong stalks. Before starting, decide how much fruit is to be used and experiment with grouping it in different numbers.
Nuts and cones Use larger varieties of nuts, such as walnuts, since smaller nuts are more difficult to attach. Fir cones can be wired to add a woody effect.
Secateurs to trim any untidy moss or foliage.
Mossing wire to attach the moss to the frame.
Stub wires are used to attach the foliage, fruit, nuts and cones to the wreath base.
Green gutta tape to disguise any visible wires.
1yd (91cm) of ribbon, made into a lavish bow, adds a professional finishing touch to the wreath.
Spices, such as cinnamon sticks, not only look good but add a wonderful, spicy fragrance.

2 Prepare the foliage by removing any smaller stems from the main branch. Trim any needles or leaves off the bottom ½in (1.2cm) of each stem. Fan out three of these smaller stems, keeping the stems together. Wind one half of a 12in (30cm) stub wire tightly around all three stems to bind them together.

3 Attach each group of three leaves to the wreath by pushing the other half of the wire vertically through the moss. Tuck the ends into the underside. (This prevents doors or surfaces being scratched when you hang up the wreath.)

6 Prepare the apples and limes by sticking two 12in (30cm) stub wires at right angles, horizontally, through the base of each fruit. Twist the ends together to form one stem and attach to the wreath base. If adding smaller fruit, such as berries, pin them in place using a hairpin or fine wire. Tightly wrap one end of a 12in (30cm) stub wire around the base of each cinnamon stick. Disguise the rest of the wire with green tape, and attach to the wreath.

7 To make the bow, hold the ribbon of your choice 3in (7.5cm) from the end, and form a small loop over your thumb. Make four large loops for the bow itself by gathering the ribbon into the middle each time. Thread the end of a stub wire through the thumb loop, around the four gathers, and twist the wire around itself. Push the wire into the wreath and bend it over on the underside to secure it.

DESIGN IDEAS

△ *Try a natural woodland theme, with Christmas roses and ivy weaving through a circle of entwined vines, and tied up with a green ribbon edged with gold.*

△ *Two rings of twisted bamboo staked together make an unusual shape. Green berries punctuate the outer ring, while red berries and cones add a seasonal touch.*

△ *Make an everlasting display from stalks of wheat spiralling around a base, with silk cornflowers and poppies pushed in at random for colour and freshness.*

△ *This wreath will look bright and festive every Christmas. Buy the base and decorate it with laurel leaves and cones, then simply spray it a rich gold.*

TIP   **ADDING DECORATIONS**

◇ Polish varnish over some areas for added lustre.

◇ If you have made a decorative base, the entire circumference of the wreath does not have to be packed with dried material. For a dynamic decorative effect, leave small areas, or even whole sections, uncovered.

◇ To add a theatrical or festive look to your wreath spray twigs gold, silver, white, or another colour of your choice.

CHAPTER III
PRESSED & DRIED FLOWERS

◇

◇

How to press flowers

Pressing is probably the most straightforward method of preserving the natural beauty of flowers. Simply by placing freshly cut blooms between sheets of absorbent paper under pressure, their moisture is absorbed, leaving a perfect two-dimensional, and often brilliantly coloured bloom.

Pressed flowers can be used to create pictures, decorate greeting cards and gift tags, make jewellery, adorn pot lids and even decorate wooden furniture. There are several methods of pressing flowers and leaves, all equally effective providing they are done properly.

The most commonly used method is to press flowers between sheets of absorbent paper (such as blotting paper) within a large book, heavily weighted with further books on top. The second method involves placing your flowers between two sheets of absorbent paper, then sliding them into the middle of a folded newspaper beneath a carpet.

The third method needs more complex equipment — a flower press. This is effectively layers of plywood which can be tightened together with four bolts — one on each corner. The flowers and paper are placed between the plywood sections, and the bolts tightened to apply maximum pressure.

There are no guidelines for the length of time flowers should remain under pressure; it is very much a matter of trial and error. Once the moisture has been absorbed by the paper the flowers are ready for use. In the case of tiny flowers the pressing need only take a couple of days. If you leave your specimens for too long, the petals will start to discolour.

It is a good idea to experiment with flowers and foliage of different types to work out approximate pressing times for each species.

◁ *Whatever the season, there is always plant material available including flowers, leaves and grasses which can be preserved by being pressed within a heavy book.*

Gathering flowers

Whether you live in the town or country, you will find an endless variety of flowers and foliage to choose from. Don't restrict yourself to the plants growing in your garden; search among the hedgerows, woods and meadows, and look for interesting grasses and foliage which grow in abundance and are essential for any pressed-flower display.

It is a good idea to familiarize yourself with the plants in your local area, particularly with any endangered species as it is now illegal to pick flowers belonging to this group. Even with common varieties, don't pick all the flower heads from one plant — careless gathering can lead to rarity in years to come.

When to pick

Always pick your flowers on a dry day once the dew has evaporated. Wet specimens will fade and can go mouldy when pressed. If you are out on a damp day and chance upon a particularly fine species, pick a couple of blooms with long stems and leave to stand in a vase of water so the dew evaporates.

It is important to press flowers as soon as possible after they have been picked — particularly wild flowers as these have a tendency to wilt after just a few minutes. Place them in sealed plastic bags, taking care not to put too many in each. Alternatively, make a travelling press in which to store your flowers while out walking.

▽ *When pressed, pansies, daisies, buttercups, larkspur, primroses and forget-me-nots will produce perfect results every time.*

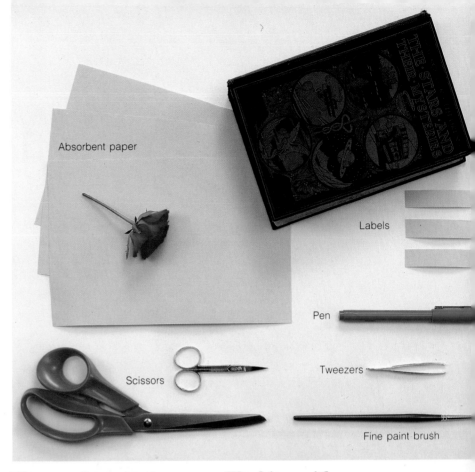

Absorbent paper

Labels

Pen

Scissors

Tweezers

Fine paint brush

Flowers for pressing

There are few flowers that cannot, with a little preparation, be successfully pressed, but simple flatish flowers such as pansies and forget-me-nots give the best results. Large fleshy flowers like roses will not press well if treated in the same way; they must be taken apart and the petals pressed separately. Others, such as foxglove and delphinium, work best when removed from their stems.

Some flowers retain their colour perfectly when pressed, others do not. Oranges and yellows are particularly good. Reds and pinks, however, sometimes lose their colour. The only way to find out what will press perfectly and what won't is to spend some time experimenting with various coloured blooms.

Working with pressed flowers

It is essential to get a good supply of flowers and foliage before you start even the smallest project. When you have pressed a large quantity, store them in separate paper or greaseproof bags, labelled for easy identification.

Work in a draughtproof room so there is no danger of the feather-light blooms being disturbed, and take care when moving your other materials around; the draught created by placing a piece of paper on the table can scatter flowers everywhere.

Once you have decided on your method of display, sketch a small plan of the basic arrangement; you can place the flowers freehand on your background, but they are frequently too delicate to move around if you change your mind.

When working with tiny flowers, such as forget-me-nots use a pair of round-ended tweezers and a small paint brush to move them around.

Use a latex-based or water-based glue rather than a clear contact adhesive; the stronger adhesives can sometimes discolour the petals.

Using a book to press flowers

1 Take your flowers by the stalks and study them carefully. Flat flowers need no preparation, but larger blooms such as roses and carnations need to be pressed petal by petal, and so should be separated before you begin.

2 Place a sheet of absorbent paper between the pages of a large, heavy book, and arrange your flowers across the page. Flowers should be of a similar thickness — any difference will cause the smaller flowers to be insufficiently weighted.

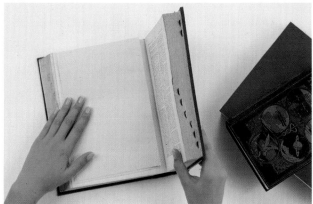

3 Place a second piece of absorbent paper on top of the flowers and gently close the book. Place the book in a position where it will be undisturbed and weight the top with a further pile of books for maximum pressure.

4 When the flowers are ready for use — this can be any time from two days to six weeks — carefully open the book and remove the specimens with round-ended tweezers, easing away gently any that are stuck to the paper.

◁ *You can make a simple travelling press out of two sheets of wood or chipboard and an old belt. Place your flowers between two sheets of thin cardboard lined with absorbent paper, then place in the press and tighten the belt.*

Preparing leaves and awkwardly shaped flowers

Cutting rosebuds Fleshy flower heads such as rosebuds can be cut lengthways, then pressed. Slice through the centre with a sharp knife and press them with the cut-side facing down.

Flattening blooms Primrose-shaped flowers have their petals joined by a small tube. For an even shape, remove the stalk, then snip off the tube with a pair of sharp scissors. Press face down.

Pressing leaves Most leaves need little preparation before pressing. Thick stalks look rather clumsy. If you feel the stalk is too thick, pare it down with a sharp knife before pressing.

Pressed-flower greetings card

Hand-made greetings cards decorated with pressed flowers are simple and satisfying to make, and their personal touch always makes them a pleasure to receive.

Sticky-backed translucent film will conserve their beauty and protect your natural posy from the damaging effects of light and air.

You will need
◇ Stiff card, 8 x 12in (20x30cm) and 4½x6in (11x15cm)
◇ Pressed flowers and leaves
◇ Latex adhesive, paint brush
◇ Sticky-back plastic
◇ Pencil, ruler and craft knife

1 Fold the large piece of card in two and mark out a 4in (10cm) x 5½in (14cm) window. Experiment with your design on the smaller piece of card.

2 Once you have decided upon your design, apply glue to the back of each flower with the paint brush and stick them in position.

3 Cut the window from the card and rub out any pencil marks. Cover the design with sticky-backed plastic then glue just inside the window.

A pressed flower picture

*An object of beauty in itself,
a pressed flower picture can evoke warm memories of summers
past and become a lasting souvenir of a
memorable holiday or day in the country, it also makes a perfect
and highly personalized gift.*

Planning the picture

The first thing to consider when planning a pressed flower picture is the flowers themselves. If you already have a selection of pressed flowers, the size, type and colour of the blooms you have available should help you to decide on the style of picture you want to make.

Alternatively, your picture may be inspired by the fresh flowers growing in your garden or in nearby hedgerows, in which case select only perfect blooms, and press as described in the previous chapter.

Choosing the background

Think carefully about the material you will use for the background as this will set the mood for the whole picture.

Fabric You can use any fabric as a backing for your picture. Cool neutral hessians, cottons and linens will create a natural country feel, while silks, velvets and brocades give your picture an opulent 'Victorian' look. Experiment with scraps of lace and ribbon to make attractive borders and bows.

Paper There is an enormous range of coloured and textured paper available which make ideal backgrounds for pressed flower designs. Handmade and marbled papers from art shops are extremely attractive and subtle enough for most pictures. Alternatively you could use scraps of wallpaper such as flock or pale watered silk for more formal structured arrangements.

◁ *This delicate posy arranged on a rich velvet background makes an ideal picture for a pretty dressing table or window shelf. Choose blooms that match the colour scheme of your bedroom for a co-ordinated look.*

Creating a design

The design of your picture must be worked out before you begin. Although you will need to experiment with the flowers and foliage to establish how the shapes and colours fit together, they are often too delicate to put up with constant handling. It is a good idea to sketch out a plan on a piece of paper before you start so you can use it as a guide when positioning your flowers.

Colour, texture and tone are as important to a picture made with pressed flowers as they are to a painting, drawing, or any other visual image. Just as the painter can bring a painting to life by careful choice of colour and composition, so the flower artist can create something special and original by being creative and using the available materials to their best advantage.

Colour Decide on a theme or colour scheme before starting your design, and try to stick to it. Obviously, your choice of colours will depend to some extent on what is available, but a little discerning choice at the outset can determine the success of the finished result.

For example, pale colours often produce a romantic picture, while warm reds and yellows make for a mellow, autumnal glow. A monochrome arrangement — a design done in various shades of one colour — has more impact than one which includes every colour of the rainbow.

All pressed flowers will mellow with time, so bear this in mind when creating a bright design. Sunlight and strong illumination both affect the natural colours causing them to fade. Where possible keep your finished picture out of direct light; this should conserve its brilliance for many years.

Texture Leaves and flowers are rich in texture, and this quality should be a considered part of your design. Although flower petals are generally smooth, they often have coloured veins or are flecked and speckled in a contrasting colour which can make them valuable elements in a composition. Foliage is enormously varied, incorporating spiky, feathery or rounded forms that provide a necessary contrast to the finer texture of many blooms. Other natural forms, such as leaf skeletons, seeds, catkins, lichens and even shells have all been successfully introduced into dried flower pictures.

Tone Tones are the light and dark areas of a picture, and these can be as important to a finished work as the actual colour. Unless you specifically want a very pale or very dark overall effect, it is generally a good idea to use a range of contrasting tones in a composition. Try placing dark shapes on light ones, and paler colours on deeper ones. This ensures that the shapes and details of the subject show up to advantage and do not merge into the colours behind them. It is helpful to have a choice of dark, light and medium coloured flowers and leaves to hand before you start to build up the picture.

Pressed flower posy picture

This beautiful posy with its subtle shades of pink and creamy white makes an ideal picture for a bedroom or pretty lounge. Follow the plan or choose your own blooms, but remember that size is important. Too many tiny blooms will make the picture look busy, while large blooms dominate the design.

You will need
◇ Picture frame
◇ Background fabric or paper
◇ Scissors
◇ Latex or water-based adhesive
◇ Ruler
◇ Pressed flowers and foliage
◇ Small paintbrush
◇ Round-ended tweezers

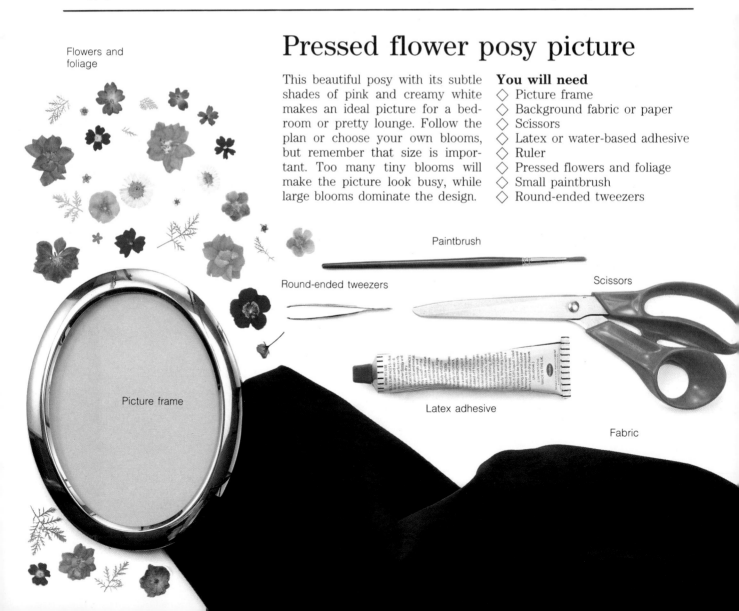

Flowers and foliage

Paintbrush

Round-ended tweezers

Scissors

Latex adhesive

Picture frame

Fabric

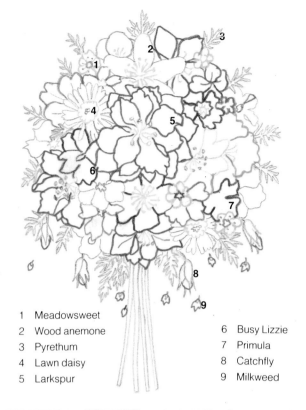

1 Cut a piece of card to the same dimensions as your picture frame. Cut a piece of fabric 1½in (4cm) larger than the frame and use it to cover the card, applying the glue to the excess fabric only (if you apply the glue to the centre of your fabric it may seep through and cause a stain). Using a ruler, measure your background lengthways and widthways to calculate the centre of the picture — this will help with the positioning of your flowers.

1	Meadowsweet		
2	Wood anemone	6	Busy Lizzie
3	Pyrethum	7	Primula
4	Lawn daisy	8	Catchfly
5	Larkspur	9	Milkweed

2 Arrange the background foliage and flowers in a circle on the fabric, following the plan, to form the basic shape of the picture. Add the next circle of flowers, which should slightly overlap the first.

3 Continue to build up the picture working from the background towards the foreground. Finally, arrange the central flower and tiny blooms to complete your design.

4 Once your picture has dried thoroughly, place it carefully inside the frame.

◆ TIP   SPRAYING AND BLEACHING

Spraying Pressed flowers can be successfully sprayed with aerosol paint for dramatic effect. White cow parsley placed against a black background conjours up the image of falling snowflakes, while gold and silver flowers and leaves add a festive touch to any picture. Spray your flowers on a large sheet of newspaper — delicate blooms may need securing with a pin to prevent them from blowing away.

Bleaching You can achieve spectacular lacy effects by applying a little household bleach to some of the more sturdy pressed flowers. Paint the petals with a mild solution of bleach then press again while still wet.

DESIGN IDEAS

△ These pressed flower miniatures have been cleverly framed with different sized wooden curtain rings. The designs themselves, set on a paper background, are made from tiny leaves in shades of green and gold, to resemble a forest in all its autumn glory.

△ ◁ This pretty circular arrangement has been built around a ring of brilliant orange rose petals set against a background of spiky green foliage. The addition of tiny flowers such as purple lobelia and cow parsley give a delicate country feel.

◁ This Japanese-style picture set — has a simple, modern feel. It is made from miniature rose leaves, cow parsley and deep red carnation petals, which were separated before pressing. The carnations have been re-arranged to form rich, lush flowers, which are set off against the pale green leaves.

Pressed flower box

*Collages of dried and pressed flowers
and foliage make an attractive decoration for the lid of a
plain wooden trinket box. The box can be lightly
stained in a colour to complement the collage or left as
natural wood to repeat the nature theme.*

Arrange pressed flowers in a lasting display on the top of a small wooden trinket box. Use this technique to decorate old wooden boxes, which can often be found at bargain prices in junk or second hand shops; alternatively, use pressed materials to add a personal touch to a plain, new wooden box.

Whether new or old, the box will benefit from being carefully painted or stained before being decorated: it is best to use a light wash of diluted water-based paint, such as acrylic or gouache. Once dressed with the floral collage, it will make a distinctive ornament or gift.

▽ *Transform a plain wooden box with a subtle wash of colour and a dainty collage of pressed flowers.*

Materials and equipment

Pressed flowers and foliage are sold by specialist suppliers. To press your own, see pages 61-68.

Adhesive Use a rubber-based or spray adhesive.

Heat-sealed transparent film This is a clear film, with one sticky side, used to seal and protect pressed flower designs. The film stretches as it is heated, so it is ideal for covering the raised surfaces of a flower collage. It is available from craft shops, as well as specialist dried and pressed flower mail order firms.

Sponge A heat resistant sponge is needed to protect the surface of the film and collage when it is ironed. Foam rubber, about ⅜in (1cm) thick is suitable.

Paints and varnish Use an oil-based paint or stain to colour the box if desired. Protect the paint or stained surface with a few coats of oil-based varnish.

Wooden boxes Unstained, natural timber boxes are available in a range of sizes and shapes. Alternatively decorate an old box.

You will need
◇ Pressed flowers and foliage
◇ Oil-based paint or stain
◇ Rubber-based adhesive (rubber cement)
◇ Tweezers and toothpick
◇ Scissors or scalpel (X-acto knife)
◇ Heat-resistant sponge
◇ Protective film (heat-sealed transparent film)
◇ Iron
◇ Oil-based varnish
◇ Wooden box

Preparation

1 Paint or stain the box to the desired colour. Alternatively leave as natural timber. Check that the box lid is completely clean and free of dust.

2 Select the plant material to be used. To plan the design, trace the size of the box lid on to a piece of paper and use tweezers to gently position the foliage and flowers on to this. Take care not to damage delicate pieces.

Working the collage

1 Apply a thin, even layer of glue to the area to be covered with the chosen pressed plant material.

2 Transfer the larger elements from the paper, picking them up with tweezers and carefully positioning them on to the glue.

3 Build up the collage by working on each area until satisfied with the density and shape of the arrangement. If any areas of floral material overlap apply a small amount of glue where necessary, to help hold the individual flowers or leaves in place.

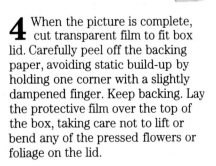

4 When the picture is complete, cut transparent film to fit box lid. Carefully peel off the backing paper, avoiding static build-up by holding one corner with a slightly dampened finger. Keep backing. Lay the protective film over the top of the box, taking care not to lift or bend any of the pressed flowers or foliage on the lid.

5 Heat iron to wool setting (110°C). Put box on ironing board and cover film with backing paper, shiny side down. Place sponge on top. Press heated iron to sponge for two minutes. If work is larger than the surface of the iron, re-position iron and hold down for further two minutes. Repeat to heat the entire surface.

◇ TIP	SEALING

If any areas look silvery after being heated, then film has not fully adhered to the surface. Reapply foam and heated iron to these areas.

6 Remove sponge and backing paper and check that film has sealed. If there are any air bubbles, prick the bubble and area around it with a fine needle. Cover with backing paper and sponge and apply iron for further two minutes.

7 Trim edges of film to fit snugly on box lid. Apply heated iron to edges, as before. Varnish sides of box with a plain or coloured varnish and allow to dry.

Preserving flowers

*By drying your own plants — whether they are
home-grown or shop-bought, you can plan the shape, colour
and texture of long-lasting flower displays.
There are three popular methods of preserving flowers and
foliage, each with their own advantages.*

◁ *The simplest method of preserving plant material is to hang it upside down to dry — and at the same time providing a floral display.*

prettier selections of flowers, grasses and foliage plants suitable for drying. Current favourites for flower arrangers include bells of Ireland, Chinese lanterns, clary sage, love-in-a-mist, strawflower, immortelles, scabious, statice, zinnia, achillea and honesty (which has transparent seed discs).

Picking the crop

Be selective when you pick grasses, foliage and flowers from your garden, making sure you leave enough to enjoy later.

Choose long-stemmed specimens and pick the best blooms as they begin to open, when their colour and condition will be at a peak, unfaded by sunlight and undamaged by wind, rain and insects.

Plants with catkins or tassels should be picked while immature, before the pollen drops. Seed pods should be picked as soon as the petals have fallen. If they are left any later, they will pepper your drying area with seeds.

Harvest your crop of flowers on sunny days when the dew has dried but before the heat has drawn too much moisture and wilted them (see page 62).

Drying and preserving

There are three traditional methods of drying and preserving flowers and foliage — air drying, steeping in a glycerine and water solution and using a drying agent or desiccant. Air drying is the most popular and traditional method of drying flowers, and is particularly suitable for plants which have a tendency to dry naturally. The glycerine method of preserving gives plants a wax quality, and can be used for quite woody and fleshy plants. Almost any plant can be desiccated — the final effect is very delicate, and the dried plants should be protected as they are very fragile. The technique can be used for complete arrangements as well as individual flowers.

The chart on page 76 will help you choose the most appropriate method of drying the most readily available plants.

Whichever method is best suited to your harvest, remove the leaves, any thorns and damaged flowers before you begin.

Growing for preserving

Quite apart from being sound economics, if you dry your own plants you will be able to enjoy the blooms, foliage and grasses while they are growing and, in many cases, during the drying process itself.

The techniques of drying flowers are neither difficult nor time-consuming — in fact, it can be highly decorative and fun. It requires a little patience, as it takes several weeks before the cut flowers are ready for arrangement. But once ready, properly dried flowers last for months or years.

What to grow

Drying flowers can capture the perfect living plant at different stages of its life cycle. It might be the bronze and golden colours of strawflowers or the full-fruited feathery seed heads of love-in-a-mist. So, when choosing which seeds to plant, remember you are looking ahead to when, like a photographer, you can snap a moment in time to preserve for seasons ahead.

Choose from a wide range of flowers specially marketed for the dried flower enthusiast. Every year the large seed firms offer wider and

Air drying

This is the simplest method of drying flowers and foliage. The aim is to allow all the moisture to dry out of the plants, while retaining as much colour and character as possible. This can be done by hanging the flowers or standing them in a vase. Some garden plants, such as bear's breeches, pampas grass, sea lavender, statice, astilbe and spiraea, dry simply and easily, placed in a vase without water in a dry, well-aired position. Others, such as larkspur, statice and roses, dry best if hung upside down. Grasses with fragile thin stems can either be hung upside down or laid flat on a sheet of newspaper or absorbent paper. If laid flat, they take a few weeks to dry and should be turned over every few days to ensure even drying.

Some plants, such as strawflowers, have stems that do not dry well. These types of flowers will be brittle and weak unless you snip the stems off and add stub wire stems to the flower heads (see page 79).

Shrubby plants, such as hydrangeas, keep their colour better if you start the drying process by standing them upright in a little water. Once this has been absorbed, do not add any more.

Flowers with fragile or wide flower heads, such as fennel or giant alliums, should be dried standing upright with their stems supported in florist's foam. The papery lantern-shaped seed cases of Chinese lanterns look more natural if dried upright, but they can also be hung upside down to dry. Leek and other allium seed heads dry just as well upright or upside down, but when standing upright the seed head has a tendency to fall into an unnatural parting.

Hanging method

To dry flowers upside down, tie bunches tightly with twine, raffia or elastic bands. (As the stems dry they become thinner and could slip out of the bunches.) Don't overcrowd the bunches — each bloom needs a free circulation of air around it to dry evenly and prevent mildew or rot spoiling them.

Hang the bunches from the rafters of a shed or garage or suspend them from a bamboo cane placed between two chairs. Keep them dry and cool (minimum temperature of 10°C (50°F) and make sure that the drying area has good air circulation. Keep flowers out of direct sunlight as this lightens their colours.

Testing for dryness

Air dried flowers are ready for use or storage from four to 10 days after picking. Test for dryness by touching gently along the stem and flower head. If the blooms are sufficiently dry, stems and petals should feel crisp. If the neck is not dry, the flower head will droop when the flowers are arranged. To avoid wasting a whole bunch stand a test flower upright in a container for a day or two. If its neck droops, wait a few days, then test another before using the bunch in a dried arrangement.

▽ *Honesty, love-in-a-mist, statice, strawflowers, gypsophila and poppy heads combine for a colourful show with interesting texture.*

Preserving in glycerine

Use a glycerine (available from chemists) and water solution to preserve woody-stemmed foliage and fleshy flowers. Flowers, such as heather, bells of Ireland and hydrangea, and sprays of foliage, such as beech, eucalyptus, ivy and mahonia, retain a flexible, natural feel when treated by this method. Colours darken slightly changing to a light straw colour or a dark mahogany brown depending on the darkness of the original pigments in the foliage.

1 Remove lower leaves of foliage stems and strip off a few inches of bark, if woody. Make a vertical cut in the stem to aid absorption and stand the cut stems in warm water for a few hours before placing in the glycerine solution.

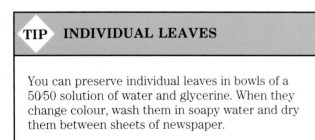

2 Prepare the preserving solution by pouring two parts by volume of nearly boiling water on to one part of liquid glycerine in a jug or heatproof container. Stir well.

TIP ▷ INDIVIDUAL LEAVES
You can preserve individual leaves in bowls of a 50/50 solution of water and glycerine. When they change colour, wash them in soapy water and dry them between sheets of newspaper.

△ *Re-create the beauty of autumn in all its glory by preserving individual leaves in glycerine.*

3 Fill another jug or heatproof container to a depth of about 4in (10cm) with the glycerine solution, taking care not to drip it on fabrics. Stand the prepared stems in the solution.

4 Place the container and plant material in a cool, dark position while the glycerine solution is absorbed. Foliage of small, thin leaves takes about a week to preserve; fleshy, larger foliage takes up to two months. Top up with solution several times during that period. When the foliage has all changed colour, the process is complete.

Desiccants

The third method of preserving flowers is by using a porous drying agent, or desiccant, to absorb moisture from the plant. This method is best suited to large flowers, such as lilies, dahlias and peonies. It is more time-consuming than air drying or preserving in glycerine, as only a few flowers can be treated at one time, but the actual drying process is relatively quick — two to six days if using silica gel, seven to ten days if using alum, borax or sand. Bear in mind, however, that unless you re-use the desiccant, it can be costly.

Silica gel crystals

You can buy silicia gel crystals from craft shops, drugstores and specialist floral sundries companies. They are relatively expensive to buy for a 'one-off' use, but they can be dried out and re-used many times. Typical packs are in 500g (just over 1lb) quantities, and you will probably need at least two packs to dry five to seven flower heads, depending on individual flower size.

If the silica gel crystals are larger than fine grains of castor sugar, you must grind them down to that consistency. Use a coffee grinder (make sure you clean it out thoroughly after such use). Alternatively, place the crystals in a strong plastic bag and crush roll them with a rolling pin.

Alum, borax and sand

Alum and borax are available from chemists and used in much the same way as silica gel.

Sand was the traditional drying agent, but ordinary sand is not as free-flowing as other desiccants, and must be cleaned and dried before use. Instead, use fine silver sand available from garden centres. Two parts of fine silver sand with three parts of alum or borax makes a suitable desiccant, but flowers will take up to ten days to dry.

▽ *Flowers dried in desiccants retain their original form and colour; but they are very fragile.*

Using drying agents

To dry flowers using desiccants you must cover them completely and keep them in an airtight plastic container until the moisture has been absorbed. Place wide-faced flowers flat on their faces; lie flower spikes on their sides and support heavy flower heads with a layer of wire mesh. Fill deep cup-shaped flowers with desiccant before you cover the whole flower.

To dry out crystals after use, place them in an even layer on a baking tray in a cool oven for up to four hours. Test that the crystals are dry using the paper humidity indicator usually sold with them. Sieve the crystals to remove unwanted pieces of plant material. Store in an airtight jar.

1 Line a large airtight tin box with a 1¼-2in (3-5cm) deep layer of desiccant. Lay a piece of chicken wire on the desiccant if drying heavy headed blooms.

2 Cut the stems off the flowers, leaving a stump about ¾in (2cm) long – once dried, you can attach an artificial stem made from wire (see page 79).

3 Sit each flower upright and spaced apart in the box. Sieve or sprinkle more desiccant over the flowers until they are covered to a depth of at least ¾in (2cm). If the container is deep enough, you can make a second layer.

4 Put the lid on the container to seal it. Stand it in a warm, dry position where it will not be moved. Test for readiness by uncovering one flower nearest the top of the box — its petals should feel papery. Don't over-dry as this causes brittleness.

Preserving flowers

Although some flowers and plants can be preserved by any of the three methods described on the previous pages, many are more suited to one particular method. The chart below looks at the most popular plants grown for drying and preserving. It indicates which part of the plant is usually preserved and the most suitable method. If you want to air dry plant material, the chart indicates whether the plant should be dried hanging (H) or upright (U) in a vase.

PLANT Name	WHAT TO PICK					HOW TO DRY		
	Bud	Opening	Full	Seed	Foliage	Air	Glycerine	Desiccant
Achillea		*				H/U		
Acrolinium		*				H		
Alium				*		U		
Artichoke		*	*			H		
Bears breeches			*			H		
Bells of Ireland		*	*				*	
Beech							*	
Chinese lantern				*		U		
Clary		*				H		
Dahlia			*			H		*
Eucalyptus					*	U	*	
Euphorbia			*			H	*	
Grasses				*				*
Hollyhock: flower			*					*
seed head				*				*
Honesty				*		H		
Hydrangea			*			U		
Jerusalem sage				*		H		
Immortelle		*				H		
Ivy		*			*	H	*	
Larkspur						H		
Lily		*	*					*
Love-in-a-mist			*	*		H		
Mahonia					*		*	
Mexican orange:						*		
foliage flower			*		*			*
Mock orange			*			U		*
Pampas grass				*		U		
Peony	*	*				H/U		*
Pansy			*					*
Rose	*	*				H		*
Rudbeckia			*					*
Scabious		*		*		H/U		
Sea lavender		*	*			H		
Statice			*			H		*
Stock			*			H/U		*
Strawflower		*	*			H		
Zinnia		*	*					*

Dried flowers

*The soft colours and delicate spicy aroma of dried
flowers bring a timeless beauty into the home. Blooms and foliage
in every colour and shade are now available and, whether you want
to make a small posy or a large decoration, you should
be able to find the flowers you need.*

An all-round flower basket

With a little skill, you can create spectacular floral displays from simple country style bouquets to sophisticated, modern table settings. With such beautiful materials, inspiration is rarely hard to find. Shades can be chosen to match your furnishings, or colours mixed to form a seasonal splash of brilliance, such as a golden mid-summer garland or a red and green Christmas posy.

You will need
- ◇ Scissors
- ◇ Craft knife
- ◇ Stub wire pins (floral pins)
- ◇ 3-4 handfuls of sphagnum moss
- ◇ Wicker basket
- ◇ Florist's foam (oasis)
- ◇ Sea lavender (*Limonium latifolium*)
- ◇ Pink everlasting flowers (*Helichrysum bracteatum*)
- ◇ Yarrow (*Achillea filipendulina*)
- ◇ Purple and pink statice (*Limonium sinuatum*)
- ◇ Love-in-a-mist (*Nigella damascena*)
- ◇ Sea holly (*Eryngium*)

Stub wire pins

Craft knife

Oasis

Sphagnum moss

Yarrow

Stub wire

Sea holly

Love-in-a-mist

Statice

Sea lavender

Everlasting flowers

Arranging the flowers

1 Cut the oasis to fit your basket, placing any left over sections on the top to create a domed shape. Take a handful of sphagnum moss and pin it all over the oasis using lengths of medium wire bent in the form of a hair pin.

2 Cut the sea lavender into sections 6-8in (15-20cm) long and create a basic dome shape. Mentally 'divide' the shape into quarters and, using small sprigs of wired yellow yarrow, highlight each one with the same number of heads.

3 Separate the bunch of purple statice into sprigs and gently insert them into your arrangement. Turn the basket as you work so that you achieve a round, even shape as defined by the sea lavender.

4 Add sprigs of pink statice, this time working across the basket in a zig-zag, from the front to the back. This is to help you to achieve a more abstract colour placement. The pink flowers should not be in circles.

5 Wire together small bunches of sea holly and love-in-a-mist seed pods, as shown below. Take each of the bunches and insert them at random into the arrangement.

6 Take the pink everlasting flowers, wire any weak stems or broken heads, then add them to the arrangement. Start at the top, inserting the flowers to form a small crown, then work downwards, turning the basket regularly.

Wiring flowers

Many dried flowers have brittle stems. These need to be wired to be used successfully.

Wiring a flower head Take a length of medium stub wire and bend one end to form a small hook. Gently feed the straight end through the centre of the flower head until the hook catches firmly in the middle of the bloom.

Wiring a sprig Separate a small sprig from a large, densely packed cluster. Place a length of stub wire through the sprig, then bend both ends down and secure by twisting around the stalk.

Wiring a spray Gather a small bunch of four or five flowers or seed heads. Bind together with a length of stub wire.

DESIGN IDEAS

Using baskets

All dried flower displays need careful planning, and the first thing to consider with any display is the container as this will determine the final shape of the arrangement. There is no need for the vessel to be waterproof, so you can use almost anything you want.

Baskets look particularly attractive; the natural wicker tones blend perfectly with the subtle shades of the flowers, but remember that small baskets must be weighted (with pebbles perhaps) so that they don't become top heavy when you start the arrangement.

◁ *This attractive cottage garden basket has been made using sprigs of pink and blue larkspur, love-in-a-mist, love-lies-bleeding, delicate pink rose buds and sweetly scented lavender. The natural clustered effect has been achieved by placing the flowers in a base of scrunched up chicken wire and sphagnum moss to give the flowers a spontaneous gathered look. The subtle blues and pinks tone beautifully with almost any colour scheme, evoking memories of summer gardens.*

▷ *Small sprigs of dried flowers can be used to make miniature arrangements to complement your large display. This tiny basket has been filled with sea lavender, love-in-a-mist and safflower, topped with a single pink straw flower. Sweet-smelling pot pourri is then scattered over the arrangement.*

▽ *Rich purple statice, sea lavender and subtle-toned everlasting flowers create an unusually brilliant splash of colour in this oyster-shaped wicker basket. A perfect display for flowers that have lost their stems.*

▽ *Pink straw flowers and delicate sprigs of sea lavender make a pretty bedroom posy or an ideal gift. This small arrangement can be made using left-over stemless flowers from larger displays.*

Dried flower garland

*Natural twisted vine wreaths can be used to
make beautiful country garlands for the home. Dressed with dried
grasses and subtle foliage, fabric-covered baubles
and bows, this wreath is an unusual decoration for a wall, fire
surround or door.*

With natural materials, you can create decorative garlands for your home. This garland was made using a twisted vine wreath and dried flowers and grasses in natural, earthy colours. Inventive additional decoration in the form of a number of fabric-covered spheres, together with a soft ribbon bow, highlight the subtle grass shades.

All the natural materials, including the wreath, are available from a florist, but you can experiment with twigs and leaves gathered from fields, hedgerows and woodlands. Put them together while fresh and leave to dry naturally before using them on the wreath.

You will need

◇ Twisted vine wreath
◇ Beech leaves (*Fagus sylvatica*)
◇ Hops (*Humulus lupulus*)
◇ Dried roses (*Rosa*)
◇ Larkspur (*Delphinium consolida*)
◇ Wheat (*Triticum vulgare*)
◇ Oats (*Avena*)
◇ Harestail grass (*Lagurus ovatus*)
◇ Love-lies-bleeding (*Amaranthus candatus*)
◇ Golden rod (*Solidago virgaurea*)
◇ Ribbon and fabric
◇ 4 table tennis balls
◇ Medium stub wire
◇ Needle and thread

Stub wire

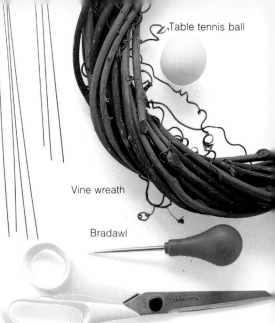

Table tennis ball

Vine wreath

Bradawl

Scissors

1 Group dried flowers, grasses and leaves separately. Then wire into small bunches using the stub wire, as shown on page 79. Use about three stems to a bunch.

Ribbon

2 Cut the fabric into about 6in (15cm) diameter circles and run a gathering thread around the edge. Wrap a circle around each table tennis ball, pull the thread tight and fasten. Cut away excess fabric.

3 Use a bradawl to punch a hole into each ball and insert the twisted wire. Then tuck the wired ends of the grasses, leaves and spheres into the wreath, binding the ends firmly around the twigs at the back.

Harestail grass

Fabric

Oats

Rose

Golden rod

Hops

4 Work the bunches and spheres into a crescent formation. Then make a bow by folding the ribbon into two figures of eight. Secure with wire and insert it at the bottom of the crescent. Add a wire hanging loop.

Beech leaves

Wheat

Larkspur

Love-lies-bleeding

Floral pomanders

*Use florists' foam and an assortment
of dried flowers and foliage to create spectacular flower-packed
floral pomanders that will deliciously scent
a room or airing cupboard. Choose flowers and foliage to
complement the existing decor of a room.*

Flower balls are built up on a round base of florists' foam — rather like making the top of a dried flower ball tree. They can be made in any size, from dainty, miniature pot pourri balls to large globes that look impressive hanging from the ceiling or rafters of a room. Here, we concentrate on small pomander-style balls.

Floral pomanders

Made on a small scale, dried floral pomanders are an attractive alternative to pot pourri sachets. They can be hung in a closet, over a coat-hanger, inside an airing cupboard or decoratively displayed looped over the corner of a dressing table. Alternatively, hang one from a wall bracket fitted above furniture or beneath a shelf.

Use large flower balls to decorate the interior of a church for a wedding. Carry the theme through to the bridesmaids, who could each carry a dainty version of the large flower ball — hanging from a silk ribbon chosen to match the colour of the dresses.

Alternatively, use a plain glass bowl or vase, slightly smaller in diameter than the finished ball, as a base on which to exhibit the floral pomander. Rest the ball on top of the container, which will form a near-invisible support.

Materials and equipment
Florists' foam

Florists' foam balls are available in various sizes, ranging from very large to small. Ball shapes can also be carved from a foam block: using a sharp knife, cut the block into a cube and then gradually slice away the foam to form a rounded shape. When deciding on the size, remember that the larger the ball, the more plant material required.

Covering the base
To form the base for the flowers, the foam ball should be completely covered. Use clumps of sphagnum moss secured in place with florists' stub wire. Alternatively, cover the foam ball with dried material, such as lavender, held with adhesive.

Suitable plants
Most types of dried flowers are suitable. For maximum impact select colourful, textured material. For a more unusual effect, try dyeing some of the plant material.

Suitable plants include broom, Cupid's dart, honesty, hydrangea, lady's mantle, love-in-a-mist, sea holly, sea lavender, statice and sweet William. Use more delicate plants, such as dill or *Gypsophila*, to soften the outline. For a defined spherical shape, decorate the ball with clusters of single flower heads, such as tiny rosebuds.

A floral pomander

Decide how the finished pomander should look before preparing the plant material. Different effects can be obtained by adjusting the length and position of the flower stems. For example, use short-stemmed flowers for a tight covering or flowers and foliage with longer stems for a loosely packed, in-formal look. Alternatively, use one type of plant material throughout for a neat, spherical shape.

The floral pomander does not have to be round — try arranging a selection of different materials in a geometric or abstract design on the round base. Finally, when choosing the ribbon, select one that will match or complement the colour of the plant materials.

You will need
◇ Dry florists' foam ball
◇ Thin gauge stub wire (stem wire)
◇ Florists' tape for helping to wire stems (optional)
◇ Wire cutters
◇ Fine wire for binding stems
◇ Sphagnum moss
◇ Fine knitting needle
◇ Selection of dried plant material
◇ General purpose glue (optional)
◇ Wide ribbon, approximately twice the diameter of the ball plus enough to make a bow
◇ Scissors

Attaching the ribbon

1 Bend a piece of stub wire in half to form a hairpin shape; twist the two ends together, leaving a loop at the top for attaching the ribbon. Push the cut ends of the wire through the centre of the dry foam ball until just the loop is showing; untwist the cut ends.

2 Using wire cutters, trim ends to a length of 1in (2.5cm); fold cut ends back and push into foam ball to secure wire and to prevent sharp ends causing injury.

3 Thread the ribbon through the wire loop at the top of the foam ball. Make sure both sides of the ribbon are of equal length, then secure it in a double knot just above the loop. Tie ends of ribbon in an attractive bow.

◁ *Red roses, champagne roses, poppy heads, husks of wheat,* Achillea *and* Amaranthus *have been combined to make this floral pomander. This combination of plant material gives a compact, rich looking pomander.*

Adding the trimmings

When decorating the foam ball, hang it above the work surface. It could be suspended from a hook in the wall, from a shelf or the top of a door. Alternatively, lay a ruler on a higher flat surface, weight one end with books and suspend the ball from the projected end. This will enable you to rotate the ball as the plant material is added to ensure that it is evenly and attractively covered with the material.

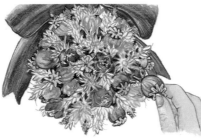

1 Follow steps 1 to 3 opposite for attaching the wire loop and ribbon. Lightly and evenly cover the foam ball with sphagnum moss; secure moss with pieces of stub wire bent into hairpin shapes.

2 To prepare the flowers, trim the stems to about 2in (5cm) long; vary the length if you want a very compact pomander or a more straggly one. Use thin gauge wire to strengthen fragile stems.

3 Bunch flower stems together into groups of three or four. Insert at intervals into the foam, covering the entire surface of the ball. With very delicate plant material, make a hole with a fine knitting needle first to avoid damaging the stems. Add a dab of glue to make sure they stay in the pierced holes.

4 Gently rotate the ball to see if there are any areas that need filling. Use colourful, bright, flowers to highlight any plain areas.

Alternative method

This floral pomander is made in a slightly different way, using adhesive to hold the plant material in place — for both the base and the decoration. Add the ribbon at the end to prevent it from becoming covered in glue.

You will need
◇ A small dry florists' foam ball
◇ About 2oz (50g) dried lavender flowers
◇ Adhesive
◇ Paint brush
◇ An assortment of dried flowers
◇ Tweezers
◇ Ribbon

Method

1 Follow steps 1 and 2 of attaching the ribbon, but do not actually thread the ribbon on to the wire loop at the top of ball.

2 Place the dried lavender flowers on a sheet of greaseproof paper. Working on a small area at a time, apply the adhesive to the foam ball with a paint brush; then, gently but firmly, roll the glued area over the lavender

flowers. Repeat this until the ball is completely covered in lavender. Leave to dry.

3 To decorate the foam ball, pick up one dried flower at a time using tweezers; dip the back in adhesive, then position on to the lavender-covered ball. Cover the entire surface attractively and completely. Leave to dry.

4 Add the ribbon — see step 3 of attaching the ribbon.

◆ TIP	FRAGRANCE

To strengthen the fragrance of a dried pomander, sprinkle it with a few drops of essential oil, such as oil of lavender, jasmine or rose.

Display care

To keep a dried pomander in good condition, replace any flowers that become damaged or faded. Use a hair dryer on a low setting to gently remove any dust or loose materials.

▽ *The flowers in this pomander have been attached with adhesive.*

DESIGN LIBRARY

▽ *Apples studded with cloves, pine needles and eucalyptus leaves are the unexpected combination for this festive decoration. Suspended from a rich red ribbon, the display would need to be sprayed with water to keep it fresh.*

△ *The subtle pinks, soft yellows and greens combined for this flower ball reflect the fact that it was made for a bridesmaid to carry at a wedding.*

▽ *Adapt the method for making a dried flower ball for fresh flowers. Here freesias, chrysanthemums, ivy, and sprigs of lavender and rosemary make a lovely, summery display.*

▷ *The two pomanders (right) were made by gluing the plant material to the foam base. The rose pomander (left) was made conventionally.*

Dried flower trees

*Dried flower trees make enchanting permanent displays
and are especially valuable for placing in dark nooks and corners
where house plants do not grow well. They are quite
simple to make and there is a wide variety of different flower
shapes and colours to choose from.*

The rich, subtle colours of dried flowers always complement one another so the colour scheme of your tree can be as varied as desired. Alternatively, a tree can look effective in a limited colour scheme — a monochromatic display of yellows and golds, for example. The tree can be made on any scale, from small to quite large.

A colourful tree

If you are drying your own flowers it is best to collect them in a good selection of colours so that you have a range of options when you are ready to make the tree. The most popular scheme for a dried flower tree uses a mixture of colours. The warm hues of deep red, burnt orange and ochre are combined with the cooling ingredients of pure white and lilac-blue.

A florist's foam cone makes an interesting alternative to using a ball. An effective idea is to copy the appearance of a cone-shaped tree such as a conifer to create a type of bonsai tree.

Once you have mastered the basic techniques of making a dried flower tree, you can experiment with other natural materials. A lovely idea, particularly as a Christmas decoration, is to cover a foam ball or cone shape with wired pine cones. You can either leave the cones natural or use gold paint to make them look even more festive and ornamental.

Striking effects can be created by using flowers in a single colour to make a simple pattern on the tree — for example, a spiral pattern around a conical tree.

Using moss

Encourage the moss around the base of your tree to stay green by mist spraying it with water.

Making the tree
You will need

◇ A plastic pot about 12in (30cm) in diameter
◇ A length of thin branch about 14in (35cm) high and 4ins (10cm) in circumference
◇ Ball of florist's foam
◇ Polyfilla
◇ Stub wires (stem wires)
◇ An attractive container
◇ Lady's mantle (Alchemilla mollis)
◇ Purple statice
◇ White statice
◇ Sea holly (Eriginium)
◇ Strawflower (Helichrysum bracteatum)
◇ Poppy seedhead (Papaver)
◇ Sea lavender (Limonium latifolium)
◇ Fresh moss

1 The finished tree is 27in (68cm) high. Use foil to line the pot and secure the length of branch inside with small stones. Mix the polyfilla into a paste and spoon into the pot until it is level with the surface.

2 Push the ball of florist's foam on to the branch to no more than half way through the foam.

3 Cut stub wires into thirds, bend the pieces over and use to pin the moss on to the foam.

Lady's mantle

Purple statice

White statice

Sea holly

Larkspur

4 Break the dried flowers off their stems to a length of about 3in (7.5cm) before you start. Push blue delphiniums, aquilegia buds and thistles into the ball first, wedging the stems in to about half way down their length.

5 Continue adding bulk and colour to the tree with lady's mantle, sea lavender and statice.

6 Complete the tree with poppy seed heads, helichrysum and red spray roses.

7 Put the tree into an attractive container such as a basketry pot. Cover the polyfilla with moss.

Red miniature roses

Strawflower

Poppy seedhead

Sea lavender

Moss

DESIGN IDEAS

▷ *A dried flower tree in shades of deep pink and red looks cheerful and the strong colour is relieved by touches of greenish yellow. A terracotta pot enhances the colour scheme and wild oats give the tree a varied outline. Moss and dried flowers are used to cover the polyfilla inside the pot, giving the finishing touch to the display.*

◁ *This tree is covered with wired pine cones to make an original display. Imitation fruit enhances the festive appearance of the tree.*

◁ *An arrangement of pink, violet and white flowers looks enchanting. And the colour scheme of the tree is complemented by its trunk, made of a bamboo stick entwined with pink ribbon.*

CHAPTER IV

CRAFTED FROM HERBS

◇

◇

Drying herbs

*Capture and preserve the wonderful
summertime aroma and flavour of your favourite herbs by picking
them at their best and leaving them to dry. You can
use dried herbs for cooking, in bath-time preparations, fragrant
sachets and pot pourri mixtures.*

Herbs offer us fragrant leaves, stems, flowers, seeds and roots to use in many ways. Although at their best when used fresh, many herbs can be preserved by drying, freezing or microwaving. You can also preserve the flavours of herbs long-term in bottles of olive or nut oils and vinegars.

When to pick

To make the most of their flavoursome properties, pick herbs early on a dry, sunny day, after the sun has dried the dew — pick them before midday when the sun's warmth will be drawing up the plants' essential oils. If you want to dry herb leaves, pick them before the plant has begun to flower, since during flowering the concentration of essential oils in the leaves is slightly lower. Cut suitable leafy stems, but only cut as much as you can handle at one time.

Many herbs can be harvested several times during the year — thyme, rosemary, sage and bay grow well all year round. Others, such as mint, tarragon and basil are not so hardy, but they may grow on a windowsill indoors. If you grow your own herbs you will not need to dry them for your own use; but you can dry them to offer as gifts to herbless friends.

Where to dry herbs

For the best results herbs need warmth, good air circulation and shade. A drying cupboard where you can stack wooden trays with

wire-mesh bases is ideal. A warm attic, an outside shed, or a shaded corner of a conservatory or porch would also be suitable.

Stand long-stemmed herbs in containers while they are drying. Tie weak-stemmed plants in bunches and hang them upside down.

A kitchen is not the ideal place to dry herbs: it is too moist, usually not well ventilated and other food aromas may swamp the fragrance of the herbs. In spite of these factors, many people choose to hang

△ *Although a kitchen is not the ideal place to dry herbs, small hanging bunches provide attractive and useful short term displays.*

their herbs in the kitchen for the short term pleasure of having the herbs conveniently close to hand whilst cooking, plus the benefit of their decorative features. Hang them in small bundles from an old-fashioned clothes-drying rack and replace the dried herbs with fresh ones as you use them.

Preparing the herbs

Herbs contain up to 70 per cent water and begin to lose moisture as soon as they are picked. To retain their essential oils at their best you must prepare them soon after picking and start the drying process as quickly as possible. Remove any dead or damaged leaves, shake off insects and, if necessary, wash and carefully pat dry with absorbent paper. Work in the shade to lessen damage by scorching sunlight.

Drying takes place gradually over a number of days. For the first 24 hours a temperature of 90°F (32°C) is best. For the rest of the drying time keep the temperature around 75°F (24°C). At these temperatures and with good ventilation in shade, herbs take up to seven days to dry. If you can't provide constant heat, the herbs will take up to two weeks to dry, but may lose some of their essential flavours.

Tie woody-stemmed herbs, such as rosemary, sage and bay, into bunches of up to ten stems. Hang them from a hook or wire coat hanger in the drying cupboard. If you have a large loft or suitable spare room, tie the bundles on to bamboo canes suspended from ceiling hooks or from a picture rail across the corner of a room.

Don't tie too many stems in each bundle. To dry the herbs evenly, air should be able to circulate around the bundles. Herbs at the centre of large bundles take longer to dry and can become mouldy.

Drying racks

Drying racks can be made using a rectangular wooden frame with small mesh wire attached to the base. To make a multi-rack drier, wire the frames to four bamboo canes. Lay the herbs down inside the frame so that they are as flat as possible and don't touch each other. Make sure there is enough space between each rack for you to reach in and handle the herbs.

Calendula flowers and rose-buds will take a few weeks to dry. Hang the rose-buds upside down in bunches and place the calendula flowers face upwards on drying racks. Remove their stems before drying. Flowers with large petals can be dried on special wire racks. The flowers are supported by the wire and their stems hang down through it.

Large seed pods can also be dried in this way: for example, the umbrella-like heads of fennel, caraway and angelica are supported by the wire mesh.

Mixed bunches

It is best to dry individual types of herbs in single bunches or in the same drying tray, as the drying times for different herbs vary. Some, such as thyme, sage, bay and rosemary, can be tied into small mixed bunches to make individual pot herb selections.

Other drying methods

Freezing is only suitable for herbs that you wish to use in cooking, such as parsley, mint, thyme and basil. Herbs dried in a microwave vary in their drying times depending on their moisture content. For example, soft, large-leaved herbs, such as mint or basil, take about three minutes.

Storing dried herbs

Once the herbs are thoroughly dry, they can be used for decorative or culinary purposes. If you do not wish to use the whole plant, remove the dried leaves from the stems and store them in air-tight jars, out of bright light.

▽ *When picking herbs to make into a decoration for your home or to give as a gift, select them for their individual colour and texture as well as for their fragrance.*

Lavender

*A favourite cottage-garden plant, lavender is
as valuable for craftwork as it is in the garden. Lovely in fresh
or dried flower arrangements, lavender is also
ideal for making pot pourris, sachets, herb pillows, cosmetics,
herbal remedies and even baskets.*

With its fragrant flower spikes in summer and aromatic, grey/green leaves, lavender has throughout history been one of the most popular of all garden shrubs. In Elizabethan times, laundresses were called lavendres as they dried their washing over lavender hedges to make it sweetly scented.

Whether grown as a formal clipped hedge or an informal, pleasantly sprawling bush, lavender embodies country garden charm. It also attracts a wide range of butterflies and bees to a garden or window box.

Lavender flowers give their name to a soft blue-lilac but the flowers actually range from deep violet-purple to pink and white. They are long lasting when cut, and excellent outline material for enlivening the silhouette of fresh or dried flower arrangements. The flower stalks may also be interwoven horizontally in wicker or vine baskets, or used upright to form the brush-like sides of lavender baskets.

Lavender's essential fragrance — fresh, warm and old-fashioned — is concentrated in the tiny calyces that surround the flowers, but the stalks and leaves are also scented.

It is possible to buy fresh or dried lavender stalks, or the dried flowers alone, but it is much more economical to grow your own lavender. Even if you do not have a garden, a window box or a container placed in a sunny spot on a patio gives enough lavender for several projects. You will then be able to make pot pourri, scented bags and other items for a fraction of the cost of buying them in shops.

Pot pourri

Lavender is a favourite ingredient of traditional pot pourris. As the flowers are so small, lavender-based pot pourris are normally enlivened with a few other dried flowers. Ideal inclusions for giving contrasting colour and texture as well as depth to the fragrance are rose petals and dried herbs, such as rosemary.

If you like the scent of pure lavender but want more visual interest, add dried helichrysum, statice and sunrays, or florets of dried larkspur, delphinium and hydrangea. Dried rosebuds, unlike dried petals gathered from fully mature blooms, have no scent and look lovely scattered over the surface of lavender pot pourri.

Accidentally broken flowers from dried flower arrangements can enliven lavender pot pourri and per-haps colour co-ordinate it to a room. Use either whole flowers or just petals; a good idea is to keep a jar in a dark cupboard for saving the odd broken flower.

Making the pot pourri

The following recipe is a basic guide for a lavender-based pot pourri. There are no absolutely right or wrong proportions for the ingredients but bear in mind that it is always better to use too little lavender oil than too much, to avoid it becoming too overpowering.

You will need
◇ 2 cups dried lavender flowers
◇ ½ cup dried rose petals
◇ 2 tbsp orris root powder*
◇ 2 tbsp dried lemon geranium leaves
◇ 2 tbsp dried rosemary
◇ 2 tbsp orris root powder
◇ ½ tsp powdered gum benzoin*
◇ 3 drops lavender oil or 2 drops lavender oil and 1 drop rose oil

* Orris root and gum benzoin powder are fixatives which prevent the fragrance fading too rapidly; they are available from some chemists, or more usually from herbalist suppliers.

Place all the ingredients except the oil in a bowl and stir gently until they are thoroughly mixed. Add the oil drop by drop, stirring all the time and then place the mixture in an airtight container, filling it to about ⅔-¾ full. Store pot

pourri in a dry, dark, warm place for 4-6 weeks and shake every few days.

Bags and sachets

Lavender-filled bags and sachets in dainty muslin, voile, lace or tana lawn have long been used to perfume linen and clothes and repel moths. Draw-string bags, tied with ribbon, or small square, round or heart-shaped sachets trimmed with lace may be filled with lavender, powdered gum benzoin and a drop of lavender oil. Alternatively, try combining equal quantities of dried lavender, thyme and lemon balm to give a delightful fragrance.

For an ideal last-minute present, fill a fine cotton, plain or mini-print handkerchief with your choice of lavender mixture, bring the corners together and tie in the middle with a bow.

Perfume clothes by tying lavender bags to padded coat hangers Make the bags from matching fabric and tie them to the hangers with ribbon, or just pour dried lavender into the tubular lining before sewing it up. You can also scent pillows with lavender by adding a handful of flower heads to the stuffing. You could also mix in petals from fully-opened roses.

Lavender boxes

There are many pretty, paper gift boxes available that can be used to make fragrant lavender boxes. Cut a piece of fine net, gauze or tulle to the shape of the top, allowing an extra ½in (1cm) to extend over the side. Fill the box up to the brim with lavender, fit the net tightly in place with a rubber band, then glue it down just above the band using quick-drying glue. When dry, snip off the band and replace it with ribbon or narrow braid.

Lavender wands

An old-fashioned lavender wand, a posy-like bunch of lavender with the flower heads wrapped in tightly woven ribbon, is also used to scent drawers and wardrobes.

Form freshly picked lavender into bunches of 7, 9, 11 or 13 stems and place a 3ft (90cm) ribbon in the centre, allowing it to extend 9in (22cm) above the flower heads. Then carefully bend the stalks back down over the flower heads and weave the long end of the ribbon horizontally between the stalks. Work from the top down until the flower heads are covered, then tie the two ends into a bow.

Herb pillows

Herb pillows help you to sleep as well as giving a delightful fragrance. They are traditionally filled with various combinations of dried lavender, camomile, rosemary, marjoram, spearmint, rose, lemon verbena and thyme. Place them under your ordinary pillows.

Lavender water

The refreshing lavender water sold at chemists is actually surgical spirit mixed with essential oil of lavender and other ingredients.

You can make lavender water by mixing 15ml of lavender oil with 375ml of surgical spirit (alcohol) and a drop of musk oil. The mixture is placed in an airtight jar, shaken every few days for two weeks and then strained through muslin into small perfume bottles. To enhance the appearance of the lavender water, place sprigs of fresh lavender upright in the bottle.

How to grow lavender

Mediterranean in origin, lavender does best in a dry, sunny position and free-draining stony or sandy soil. If you are growing lavender in a large container or window box, mix the potting compost with peat or coarse sand. Heavy, waterlogged or very rich soil is unsuitable. Although lavender is moderately hardy, some species, such as French lavender (*Lavandula stoechas*) need extra winter protection.

Dwarf forms, such as Hidcote or Nana, make excellent hedges for paths, borders or herb gardens, or mini-hedges for sunny window boxes. Lavender is ideal for sunny patios where the reflected heat from the paving intensifies its fragrance.

Lavender needs little care once it is established. It flowers profusely in summer; if you don't harvest the flowers, deadhead after flowering and trim hedges lightly. In spring, cut out frost-damaged growth. Old, leggy plants can easily be replaced with semi-ripe cuttings taken in midsummer. Harvest lavender just as the flowers start to open.

Other lavender products

Lavender is used for beauty products and is an ideal ingredient for bath sachets and essences because of its relaxing aroma.

Lavender soap balls can be made from lavender water and unscented, good-quality soft white

soap. Grate a large bar into thin strips. Heat 60ml (¼ cup) lavender water and pour over the soap. Leave for 10 minutes, stir, then place in a blender, adding 3 drops of lavender oil. Cool and pour into a pudding basin. Leave 2-3 days, or until the soap begins to dry out, then form into balls and place on a sunny windowsill to dry. When almost dry, dip your hands in lavender water and rub the ball to make it smooth.

Lavender bath sachets are ideal for soothing aches and pains. Place 2 tablespoons each of dried lavender flowers and rosemary in a muslin bag with a spoonful of epsom salts. Hang the bag under the hot water tap, looped on a long string or place it directly in the water. Dry between use and discard once the scent fades.

Lavender hair rinse adds shine to your hair. It is made by boiling a handful of flowers and stalks in a pint of water. Cool, strain and pour into a bottle.

Lavender vinegar is therapeutic and, if dabbed on the forehead, helps to relieve headaches. Using a jar or bottle, steep a few sprays in white vinegar. Place the container in a sunny spot, shake daily and replace with fresh flowers after a week. Repeat for a further week, then strain through muslin and bottle. Another remedy for headaches is 2-3 drops of lavender oil taken on a sugar cube.

Lavender sugar is made of a few bruised spikes sealed in an airtight jar with sugar. The sugar can then be used to give sponges and icings a lovely scent.

Lavender-scented candles are made by adding a few drops of lavender oil to melted wax before moulding.

Potpourri

Pot pourri is as popular for its beautiful colour and texture as for its fragrance. Many shops now carry a good choice of reasonably priced pot pourri, but it is easy to make your own mixture, with flowers and foliage from the garden, ready dried material from shops or a combination of both.

Pot pourri is French for 'rotten pot', and gets its name from a fermented, layered mixture of petals, salt, spices and fixatives. In medieval times, this unsavoury looking but fragrant substance was kept in perforated or lidded pots, and used to mask unpleasant smells and to ward off diseases.

Today, old-fashioned, or moist, pot pourri has largely been replaced by dry pot pourri, which is easier and quicker to make and far more attractive, since the petals keep much of their original colour and form. Its scent is not as intense or long lasting as the moist style of pot pourri, but dry pot pourri with jaded scent can be refreshed by adding essential oils or ready-mixed essences.

In the box from left to right, top to bottom: cloves; rosebuds; lemon verbena; white statice; hibiscus; dried orris root powder; wood shavings; lavender; rose petals.

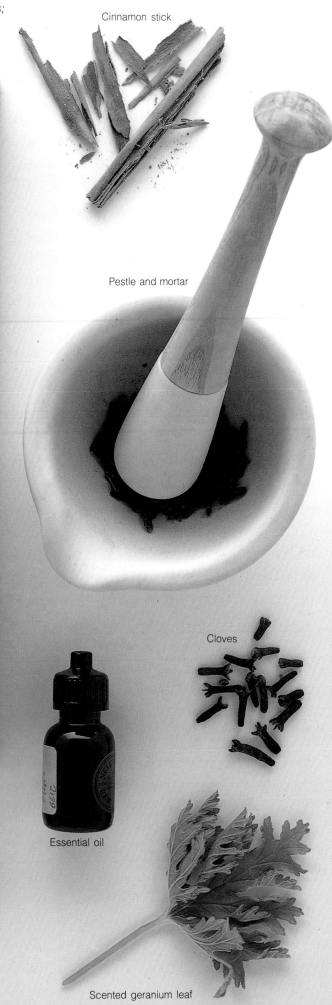

Cinnamon stick

Pestle and mortar

Cloves

Essential oil

Dried lemon peel

Scented geranium leaf

Why make your own?

Making pot pourri is a satisfying leisurely hobby that you can pursue as and when time allows. It is an excuse to get out in the garden and to keep in touch with nature. Though summer is the main season for collecting material, there are flowers for drying all year round.

Although there are many recipes, the ingredients fall into four main categories: flowers for scent or colour; aromatic leaves and herbs, which also add bulk; spices and citrus peel to sharpen the pot pourri's floral scent; fixatives to preserve the blend.

Once you are familiar with these basics, you can vary a recipe by adding essential oils to intensify a favourite scent or by introducing seed heads, bark, cones or wood shavings for visual interest. Display the mixture in a bowl or use it as the basis for herb pillows or scented sachets.

Materials

Flowers, leaves and herbs

Make sure that all plant material is thoroughly dry before making up the pot pourri.

Spices

Cinnamon, nutmeg, mace, cloves and allspice are traditional, but anise, cardamom, root ginger, coriander and vanilla pods are sometimes used in exotic mixes. Freshly ground or grated spices have a stronger, clearer aroma than ones bought as powders. Cinnamon sticks, allspice and juniper berries are sometimes used whole, for textural interest.

Dried citrus peel

Traditionally, oranges and lemons are used to add a refreshingly sharp contrast to floral scents, but limes, grapefruit or satsumas are also fine. Use thin-skinned fruit, or use a sharp knife or potato peeler to remove the skin with a minimum of pith attached. Dry flat, as previously described.

Fixatives

These are used to absorb, blend and preserve the scent of dried flowers, herbs, spices and oils. Musk, ambergris and civet are traditional fixatives, but today gum benzoin, in resinous form, or powdered dried orris root, the root of *Iris florentina* are used. Both are sold by herbalists and some chemists; orris root has a lovely violet scent of its own.

Essential oils

Rose, lavender, lily-of-the-valley, rose geranium, sandalwood, lemon verbena, almond, gardenia, cedarwood, eucalyptus and citronella oils are sold at many chemists and body-care shops. Use them sparingly to enhance pot pourri.

What to pick

For fragrance: Provence roses; damask roses; lavender; wallflower; chamomile; verbena; tansy; sweet woodruff; hyacinth; heliotrope; narcissus; clove pink; tobacco plant; cotton lavender; sweet violet; lilac; sweet pea; mock orange; freesia; mimosa; lime blossom; mignonette; jasmine; honeysuckle.

For colour: florist's roses; unopened rosebuds; zinnia; clematis; hydrangea; golden rod; larkspur; calendula; delphinium; peony; helipterum; cockscomb; marigold; pansy; mallow; nasturtium; campion; borage; globe amaranth; heather; yarrow; statice; buttercup; helichrysum; hibiscus.

For bulk and aroma: lemon verbena; rosemary; scented-leaved geranium; lemon balm; lemon thyme; artemisia; sweet basil; sweet marjoram; costmary; bay; bergamot; myrtle; tarragon; dill; sage; various mints.

Picking and drying

Try to pick all flowers, buds, leaves and herbs on a dry morning, after the dew evaporates but before the sun's heat evaporates volatile oils, the source of plants' scent. Plants that are picked wet from rain or dew are liable to rot. Flowers are most fragrant when fully open, and herbs are most aromatic when starting to flower.

Dry material as soon as possible after picking, and treat each type of flower and leaf separately, or place them on separate areas of paper, since drying times vary.

Drying whole stems

You can air-dry small flowers by hanging the stems upside down in small bunches in a dry, dark, well-ventilated spot, such as an attic. Once the petals are papery and crisp, carefully snip the heads from the stems.

Drying small flowers

Alternatively, snip small fresh flowers where they join the stems and dry in a single layer on a sheet of kitchen paper, placed on a wire mesh screen or baking rack so that the air can circulate. Place in an airing cupboard, on top of a night-storage heater, or other warm, dry, dark spot, for about a week, turning them over once or twice. With larger flowers, carefully remove the petals and dry in a single layer in the same way.

Drying leaves

Leaves can be air-dried on their stems, as above, then stripped from the stems when dry. Alternatively, strip the fresh leaves from their stems, tearing larger leaves into pieces, then dry on kitchen paper.

A traditional pot pourri

This recipe gives a fresh, floral mixture, balanced by the sharpness of lemon and scented geranium.

You will need
◇ 1 cup each dried rose petals and lavender
◇ ½ cup each dried rosebuds, lemon verbena leaves and scented-leaf geranium leaves
◇ 1 strip dried lemon peel
◇ 1 tsp allspice berries
◇ 1½ tsp cloves
◇ 1 cinnamon stick
◇ 2 tsp dried orris root powder
◇ 2 drops rose oil
◇ Scissors
◇ Pestle and mortar
◇ Lidded jar

▽ *Show off the texture and colour of pot pourri by displaying it in glass containers.*

1 Mix the dried petals, buds, lavender and leaves in a large bowl. Using the scissors, cut the lemon peel into small pieces, and add to the bowl.

2 Using a pestle and mortar, crush the allspice berries and cloves. Break the cinnamon stick into small pieces. Add all the spices and mix thoroughly.

3 Sprinkle the orris root powder over the ingredients and mix thoroughly. Add the rose oil, and mix again.

4 Place in the lidded jar and store for four weeks, shaking or gently stirring the mixture every few days. Display in a glass container, a basket or use in scented sachets.

Moist pot pourri
Dry six cups of fragrant rose petals until leathery: two to three days in a warm, dry, airy spot. Combine ¼ cup coarse salt and ¼ cup table salt. Using a 2pt (1 litre) wide-necked ceramic jar, place the petals, in ½in (1.2cm) thick layers, between layers of salt. Place, uncovered, in a dry, airy spot for 10 days, stirring daily.

When the mixture is dry and caked, crumble gently and add ½ tsp ground cinnamon, 3 dried lemon verbena leaves, ½ tsp ground cloves, ¼ cup dried lavender, 1 tbsp dried orris root powder, ½ cup dried rose buds and 2 heaped tbsp dried rosemary. Cover and leave for six weeks to ferment.

Sachet mixtures

*Capture the essence of a summer garden with
a fragrant and colourful mixture of dried flowers and leaves.
Fill small sachets — 'sweet sacks' — with sweetly
scented flower petals, tangy spices and aromatic herbs and use
them to scent rooms, bed linen and clothes.*

For centuries, small sachets of dried herbs and flowers have been used to keep clothes and linen smelling sweet and free from moths. All the ingredients in the mixture must be completely dry before being used to fill sachets.

Sweet sack fillings

The basic ingredients for a sweet sack filling are dried herbs and flowers plus a selection of spices, dried orange or lemon peel, orris root powder and essential oils.

Aromatic leaves

Select fragrant leaves which will blend in with the scent of the chosen flowers. The leaves should be dried whole and then broken up to release their scent before they are added to the blend.

Suitable leaves include: alecost, basil, bay, bergamot, feverfew, hyssop, lemon balm, lemon verbena, melilot, various mints, mugwort, scented *pelargoniums*, rosemary, sage, southernwood, sweet-briar, tansy, tarragon and thyme.

Flowers for scent

Flowers with long-lasting scents, such as lavender and violets, are ideal. For fragrance, select whole flowers before they open fully.

Other suitable flowers include: *acacia*, carnations, elder, *freesias*, honeysuckle, jasmine, lily-of-the-valley, *narcissus*, orange blossom, roses, stocks and wallflowers.

▽ *When making a sweet sack,
select petals, leaves and spices for
their combined fragrances.*

Spices, peel and roots

Because of their strong aroma, spices, citrus peels and roots should be used sparingly in sweet sack mixtures. A proportion of about 1tbsp of ground spice, citrus peel or roots to 2oz (50g) of flowers and leaves is advised. When combining spices in a mixture, use equal quantities of each.

The best scent is obtained by grinding or grating whole, fresh spices. To make dried citrus peel, cut a thin layer of peel and then dip it in orris root powder to intensify the scent; leave the peel to dry slowly. Roots need to be cleaned, peeled and sliced; leave them to dry slowly, then chop or crush them to release their scent.

Any of the following work well in sweet sack mixtures: allspice, aniseed, cinnamon, cloves, dill seed, ginger, juniper, nutmeg, vanilla pods; dried peel of all citrus fruits; roots of angelica, cowslip, sweet flag and valerian.

Fixing the scent

In order to make scents longer-lasting it is necessary to add a fixative powder. Orris root is the most popular fixative as its sweet violet scent does not strongly affect the aroma of a mixture: use about 1tbsp per 1oz (25g) of blended flowers and leaves.

Essential oils

Essential oils are ideal for adding strength and depth of fragrance to a mixture. They can also be used to revive an old mixture which has lost its scent; add only a few drops to each mixture or it will overpower the existing fragrance.

▽ *Loosely fill the sachets and secure with a piece of ribbon.*

Basic method

Decide where the sweet bag is to be used and choose appropriate flowers, herbs and spices.

1 Make sure all the ingredients are crisply dry before you start. Finely crumble them into a bowl, taking care not to reduce them to dust.

2 Crush the spices and add to the bowl. If using citrus peel as well, this should also be crushed before adding to the bowl. Add the orris root and mix together well.

△ *Hang bunches of flowers and herbs to dry before adding them to a mix.*

3 Add the essential oils if desired, a drop at a time, stirring between each drop.

4 Put the mixture into a polythene bag. Seal the top and leave for six weeks to mature.

5 Use the matured mixture to fill sweet bags. Pack the bags fairly loosely to allow the fragrance of the herb mixtures to be more easily released.

Lavender and herb mixture

This fresh, spicy mixture is ideal for scenting clothing, sheets and towels.

You will need
◇ 2oz (50g) dried lavender flowers
◇ 1oz (25g) dried lemon verbena
◇ ½oz (15g) each of dried peppermint and dried rosemary
◇ 2tbsp cloves, crushed
◇ 2tbsp cinnamon stick, crushed
◇ 2tbsp orris root powder
◇ 4 drops lavender oil
◇ 2 drops each of lemon verbena and peppermint oil

Sweet rose mixture

This sweet sack mixture has a soft, luxuriant scent that is perfect for placing amongst your personal linen and summer clothes. Blend all the ingredients together, by following the steps for the basic method.

You will need
◇ 2oz (50g) dried rose petals
◇ 1oz (25g) dried marjoram
◇ 1oz (25g) dried lavender flowers
◇ 2tbsp dried orange peel, crushed
◇ 2tbsp orris root powder
◇ 4 drops rose oil
◇ 2 drops lavender oil

Fragrant pomanders

*Pomanders combine the spicy fragrance of
cloves with the tangy sweetness of citrus fruits to produce a
wonderfully aromatic and decorative object.
Deliciously scented, they can sweetly scent a room or linen and,
more importantly, will mask unpleasant odours.*

Capture the fresh scents of fruits
and herbs by making a pomander
from citrus fruit decorated with
whole cloves. Once the fruit has
completely dried its deliciously
spicy, citrus aroma lasts for months.

Materials and equipment

Citrus fruit has been traditionally
used as the base of the pomander.
Other fruit, such as apples, can be
used, but these will bruise and
shrivel more than citrus fruits.
Darning needle is used for pricking holes in the skin.
Cloves with strong stems and large
heads to stick into the skin.
Spices are lightly dusted over the
fruit to make it more fragrant.
Orris root powder is used to help
fix and preserve the various scents.
Grooving tool is used to carefully
cut out the pattern on the skin.
Paper bag to wrap up the pomander, while it is placed away to dry.
You will also need, **greaseproof
paper, ribbons, pins, sequins,**
and a **felt tip pen.**

Design ideas

Before planning your design, remember that the fruit will shrink to
about two-thirds of its original size
during the slow drying process.

Partially cover the pomander
with cloves in a random pattern or
form a more controlled design by
carving a pattern first with a grooving tool. Whichever you choose, remember to leave space between
each clove to allow for shrinkage.

To use the grooving method:
Mark a design with a felt tip pen
then follow this pattern with a
grooving tool — chisel lightly into the
skin. Stick the cloves in the grooves.

◁ *Follow the natural curve of citrus
fruit when marking a design with a
grooving tool.*

You will need

- ◇ A large, thin-skinned orange, lemon or lime
- ◇ About 50g (2oz) of whole cloves
- ◇ 2tsp ground cinnamon (or your favourite spice)
- ◇ 2tsp orris root powder
- ◇ Darning needle
- ◇ Greaseproof paper
- ◇ Paper bag
- ◇ Ribbon and sequins (optional)
- ◇ Small grooving tool (optional)
- ◇ Felt tip pen (optional)
- ◇ Lemon juice

Method

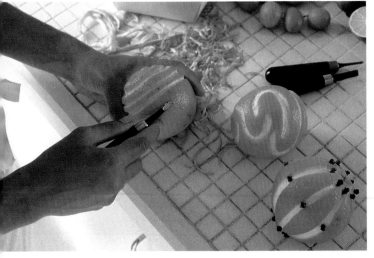

1 Gently knead the skin to soften it. If you wish, mark and groove a pattern on the skin. Rub the pith with lemon juice to keep it shiny.

▽ *Attach ribbon and lace trims with strong glue or pins pushed into the pomander.*

2 Stick the whole cloves into the fruit, pricking the skin with a darning needle first if necessary. Leave a clove space between each to allow for any shrinkage as the fruit dries.

3 Mix the orris root powder with the spices — you could use cinnamon, grated nutmeg, coriander, or any other favourite spice. Put the mixture on to a sheet of greaseproof paper. Gently roll the decorated fruit in the spices and powder mix, until it is evenly coated.

Drying

Wrap the finished fruit in a paper bag and leave in a dark, dry, airy place for at least three weeks. It should dry thoroughly, shrink and harden. The fruit must dry completely or it will go mouldy.

Trims

Once the fruit has dried add the finishing decorative touches. Tie it with ribbon, lace or coloured net. To hang the pomander up — make a loop of ribbon and secure with glue or pins.

◇ **TIP**	**SCENT**

The fragrance of a pomander should last for many years. But if the scent begins to fade, refresh the perfume by lightly painting the pomander with an aromatic oil — such as orange essence mixed with cloves. This will produce a wonderfully sensual, tropical smell of citrus and spices. Place the pomander in a warm place (between 18 and 22°C, 65-70°F), where the scent will smell strongest.

Essential oils

Besides giving great pleasure in fragrant and aromatic gardens, essential oils can also be extracted from the plants. Essential oils have been used for thousands of years — not only for their aromatic properties, but also for use in medicinal and cosmetic preparations.

Just as each individual has his or her own unique characteristics, so does each species of plant. This is partly shown in the colour of the flower and the size and shape of the leaves. However, it is the essential oil contained within that gives a plant its unique fragrance — which can range from being very strong to barely detectable. Essential oils are made up of a number of chemical compounds, the most common being esters — a combination of an acid and an alcohol.

Source of the oil

There are many fragrant plants growing all over the world and essential oils can be extracted from most of them. The part of the plant used is that which has the highest concentration of oil.

The oil from petals is called an attar. It is extracted from the scented flowers of a typical English garden, such as rose, wallflower, carnation and jasmine. In certain plants, in particular the clove, the buds contain more oil than the open flower, so the buds are harvested for aromatic and culinary use.

Herbaceous plants, such as rosemary, lemon balm and the scented pelargoniums provide oil from their leaves. Some plants with faintly aromatic foliage and flowers have highly scented roots or rhizomes. These range from the exotic ginger of the east to the iris, roseroot and geranium of our own gardens. Oils are also extracted from citrus fruits, such as lemon, orange and lime.

Many plants are grown for their seeds which are used as spices. Oils can be extracted from many of these, such as cumin, cardamom, fennel and nutmeg. Trees and shrubs also provide oils which are extracted from their barks, woods and resins. For example, cedarwood and sandalwood oils are taken from the bark and wood; storax, myrrh and frankincense oils come from resins.

Whichever part of the plant the oil is taken from, the actual amount of oil produced is exceedingly small but highly concentrated. However, a little essential oil will go a long way.

Producing oils

There are three main methods by which essential oils are extracted from plants commercially — by expression, distillation and extraction.

Expression
This method is said to produce the finest quality oils, which are often the most expensive to buy. The plants are subjected to a high degree of pressure and the oil is literally squeezed out. No heat is applied during this process, so the final product is very near to its natural state. Expressed oils are sometimes referred to as cold-pressed oils.

▽ *The essential oil extracted from the leaves of scented pelargoniums has a delightfully light perfume. The oil is often used in aromatherapy.*

Distillation
This method has been used in Turkey for thousands of years. The plants are put in boiling water so that the essential oil evaporates into the steam. As the steam condenses the liquid is collected and left to stand. The oil floats to the surface and is skimmed off.

Extraction
This process is much simpler and there are two basic methods, enfleurage and maceration. Both work on the principle that one oil will attract another to itself. It is these two methods that can be most easily adapted for use in the home.

Enfleurage This involves steeping the plants in cool olive oil. After a time, the oil is strained off and the plants are replaced with fresh ones. This process is repeated until the scent of the oil reaches the required strength.

Maceration works in a similar way, except that the container of oil is placed in hot water for a few hours each day to speed up the process.

Making essential oils

The key to making your own essential oils is in the choice of plant materials — on the following page you will find some suggestions. Little in the way of equipment is needed, other than jars and saucepans which you will probably already have in the kitchen.

△ Fresh leaves from herbs such as tarragon, thyme and lemon balm are best gathered in the morning — after the dew has dried and just before the flowers open.

Plant materials

Oils to use
Use a refined oil to attract the essential oil from the plant. Choose one that has a pale colour and mild scent — olive, safflower and sesame oils all work well.

Flowers to use
Choose from any of the following: roses, pinks and carnations, violets, wallflowers, lilac, jasmine, hawthorn flowers, lavender, honeysuckle, hyacinth, orange blossom, lily of the valley, sweet pea and heliotrope. Cut the flowers just before they are fully open and, where possible, use the petals only. Use a single type of flower, or mixtures of two or more together. The flowers can also be mixed with small amounts of herbs, such as lavender or marjoram.

Leaves to use
Almost any garden herb can be used to make essential oils. Cut the herbs just before the flowers open; use the leaves and flowers, but not the woody stems. Chop the leaves before adding them to the oil. Treat the leaves of scented pelargoniums in the same way.

Recommended herbs are the many varieties of frag-rant thyme, marjoram, peppermint, lemon verbena, lemon balm and rosemary. If making an essential oil for culinary purposes add sage and fennel.

Spices to use
Cinnamon, nutmeg (grated), cloves, cumin and coriander are best for home-produced oils. Use a pestle and mortar to crush them before adding them to the oil.

Citrus peels
The zest of citrus fruits, pared very thinly, can also be used to make essential oils. Use them very sparingly in mixtures — about two strips of zest per bottle.

Mixing plant materials
The plant materials can all be used singly or they can be mixed to make oils that are useful in pot pourri and other scented craft items. When mixing different plant materials, use at least twice as many flowers as herbs and only small amounts of the spices and peels. The mixtures can be varied to suit final use, personal taste and availability. The following mixtures work particularly well when mixed together.
◇ Rose, pinks, honeysuckle, nutmeg.
◇ Rose, lavender, cinnamon, nutmeg, orange peel.
◇ Rose, jasmine, coriander, lime peel.
◇ Rose, marjoram, lemon verbena, lemon peel, cinnamon.
◇ Lavender, peppermint, lemon balm and peel, marjoram.
◇ Violet, hawthorn, lily of the valley, cinnamon.

▽ Sweet peas should be cut just before noon on a dry, sunny day when the flowers are almost fully open, taking care not to bruise the oil-rich petals.

The basic essential oil

The easiest methods by which to make your own essential oil are by enfleurage and maceration. In a long, sunny summer, there will be no need to heat the oil. But in dull weather, or if you are making a spice oil in winter, maceration in warm water will have to be employed.

You will need

◇ 1pt (600ml) wide-necked jar with tight-fitting lid
◇ ½pt (300ml) oil
◇ 8tbsp flower petals (either a single variety or a special mixture); or 6tbsp chopped herbs; or 4tbsp crushed spices; or 6tbsp thinly pared citrus zest. In each case, the amount of plant material needs to be renewed nine times
◇ Glass or pottery mixing bowl
◇ Muslin (to cover the top of the bowl)
◇ Brown or green glass bottle with tight-fitting lid or stopper

1 Put the oil into the jar; then add the plant material and stir. Cover tightly and leave on a sunny windowsill for 48 hours, shaking every 12 hours.

2 Lay the piece of muslin over the bowl and strain the oil through it. Gather up the muslin and squeeze the plant material to extract as much oil as possible.

3 Return the oil to the jar and add fresh plant material. Continue in the same way until ten amounts of plant material have been soaked in the oil.

4 If the weather is cold and dull, stand the jar in a saucepan of cold water. Slowly heat the pan until the water is just hand-hot. Keep at this temperature for 10 minutes. Remove the jar. Do this once a day.

5 After the final straining and squeezing, strain the oil for a final time through clean muslin to remove any tiny particles that might have been squeezed through.

6 Store the oil in a dark coloured glass bottle. Keep it airtight by covering with a tight fitting lid or stopper.

Uses of essential oils

Essential oils are added to pot pourris to enhance and give a more lasting effect to the natural fragrances of the flower and herb ingredients. For the same reasons fragrant oils are added to filling mixtures for herb sachets and pillows. To make a strongly scented fruit pomander it is a good idea to soak the cloves in a fragrant oil before arranging them in the fruit. Essential oils can also be painted over pine cones and dried flower arrangements to add a stronger scent.

To remove unpleasant smells from rooms, boil a small amount of water containing a few drops of essential oil. Alternatively, put the oil into a vaporiser that is fixed over a candle or around a light bulb.

Cotton wool dipped in an essential oil can be rubbed on the inside of drawers or over wrapping paper. Or drop a little oil on to a duster before polishing to give a slight fragrance to furniture.

Naturally made essential oils can be added to spring water to make washes for the face and hands, or added to soaps and other toilet preparations.

Many oils have healing properties and are used in aromatherapy and massage. They are also used in cough remedies and medicines. Some oils are also used as natural flavourings in food and drink. Use home made herb oils in salad dressings; add peppermint oil to sweets; or use lemon oil to flavour cakes. Earl Grey tea is flavoured with the oil of the bergamot orange.

Soothing herbal baths

*Lie back and relax in a deliciously scented
herbal bath, prepared at home using only the purest ingredients.
Try herbal infusions, bath and washing bags and
special vinegars and bath oils made with herbs chosen for their
restorative, relaxing and invigorating qualities.*

Water has curative powers and, when you are feeling tired or tense or your limbs are stiff from exercise, a long soak in a warm bath is an excellent restorative. Herbs can help to increase the healing process: they can make a bath soothing, reviving, stimulating, or calming. They also have emollient, tonic and deodorizing properties which go to work as you relax.

Using herbs in the bath

There are four main types of herbal bath preparations: herbal decoctions or infusions, herbal bags, herbal vinegars and bath oils. Never add herbs straight to the bath water as they can clog the plug hole and will also stick to you, making drying a rather messy business!

The bath water should be hot enough to release the herbal essences but not hot enough to burn your skin or sap your energy. Place a cushion under your head and relax for at least 15 minutes. Dry yourself with a warm, rough towel.

Mixing herbs

Herbs can be used singly or mixed, which enables you to combine different herbal properties to obtain the effect that you need. Mixed herbs also give a more complex and pleasing scent. Experiment to find your ideal mixture.

Herbal bath infusions

Herbal infusions for the bath need to be concentrated as they are mixed with a large volume of water.

You will need
◇ 2oz (50g) dried or 4oz (100g) fresh herbs of your choice
◇ 1pt (600ml) boiling water
◇ Jug with cover
◇ Sieve

1 Put the selected herbs of your choice into the jug and pour boiling water over them. Cover jug immediately and leave to infuse for at least 30 minutes.

2 Strain infusion through a sieve, and add it to the bath water after turning off the taps.

Herbal decoction

This decoction contains bran which helps to soften the water.

You will need
◇ 2oz (50g) dried or 4oz (100g) fresh herbs of your choice

Bath herbs	Properties
Basil	Tonic; deodorant
Bay	Soothes aching limbs
Bergamot	Tonic; soothes aching limbs
Blackberry leaves	Invigorating
Chamomile	Calms nerves; soothes skin
Elder flowers	Relaxing; emollient
Hyssop	Relaxing; relieves rheumatic pains and stiffness after sport
Lavender	Refreshing; relaxing; a powerful natural disinfectant
Lemon balm	Refreshing; soothing; tonic
Lemon verbena	Refreshing; relaxing; often used for its scent
Lime flowers	Relaxing; an old folk remedy for hysteria; emollient
Lovage	Natural deodorant
Marjoram	Calming; eases rheumatic pains
Meadowsweet	Relaxing; eases tired limbs; smells like new-mown hay
Mint	Refreshing; relaxing
Mugwort	Eases fatigue; restores suppleness to stiff limbs
Pennyroyal	Refreshing; enlivening
Raspberry leaves	Tonic and slightly astringent
Rose	Use with other herbs for its scent
Rosemary	Relieves tired limbs and relaxes aching muscles; tonic; firms the skin; soothes tired nerves. This has the strongest, most penetrating scent of all bath herbs. Its properties can be released by holding several sprigs of young tips under hot running water
Sage	Cleansing; enlivening
Thyme	Cleansing
Valerian	Soothing and sedative; use with other more fragrant herbs as it has a bitter aroma

◇ 1oz (25g) bran
◇ 1¹⁄₂pts (900ml) boiling water
◇ Enamel or stainless steel saucepan with lid
◇ Sieve

1 Put the herbs and bran into a saucepan with the water and bring them gently to the boil. Cover and leave to simmer for about 30 minutes.

2 Strain the mixture through a sieve and use in the same way as for the herbal infusion.

Bath bags

Muslin, calico or thin, plain cotton can be quickly stitched into simple bags which can then be filled with dried herbs. Other finer-textured ingredients can also be added in equal proportions to the herbs. For example, add cornmeal to cleanse or ground almonds to soften the skin. Make several bags at a time.

You will need
For each bath bag:
◇ Fabric bag, approximately 4 x 3in (10 x 7.5cm) square
◇ 2tbsp dried herbal mixture
◇ 20in (50cm) string or piping cord

Fill the bag with the herbal mixture. Tie the string round the top of the bag, making a loop for the bag to hang by. To use, tie the filled herbal bath bag to the hot tap so that it hangs in the stream of hot running water. Alternatively, hang it under the shower spray to achieve a similar beneficial effect.

Washing bags

Washing bags contain a mixture of herbs and cornmeal. Rub them over your skin to cleanse and smooth away dead cells.

▷ *Bath bags are simple to make and effective to use.*

To make a washing bag

Put 4tbsp dried herbs and 2tbsp cornmeal in a muslin bag, 4 x 3in (10 x 7.5cm) square. Sew up end. To use, place the bag under the running taps. Rub it over your arms, legs, neck and back while you are in the bath.

Bath vinegars

Herbal bath vinegars help to soften both the water and your skin. The following recipe makes enough herbal vinegar for two baths.

You will need

◇ ½pt (300ml) light coloured cider vinegar
◇ ½pt (300ml) spring water
◇ 1oz (25g) dried or 2oz (50g) fresh herbs of your choice
◇ Stainless steel or enamel saucepan
◇ Bowl with cover or clingfilm
◇ Sieve
◇ Bottle

1 Put the cider vinegar, spring water and your chosen herbs into the saucepan. Then gently heat the mixture to simmering point, but do not boil.

2 Take the pan from the heat. Pour the vinegar mixture and herbs into a bowl and cover. Leave mixture for approximately 12 hours, then strain and bottle it.

Bath oil

Bath oils can be made with home-made or bought essential oils and Turkey Red oil, a specially treated castor oil available from chemists and herbalists. If you cannot obtain Turkey Red oil, use almond, avocado, sesame or olive oil, and add 1 teaspoon of vodka or brandy to aid dispersal. For making essential oils see pages 107-110.

To make the bath oil

Put 1tbsp of Turkey Red oil into a small, dark bottle and add 1tsp of essential oil (use a single type or a mixture of two). Cover tightly and shake well. Store for two weeks. To use, add 1tsp to running water.

Foot baths

Relaxing with your feet in a warm herbal foot bath will help to refresh and restore your whole body. You will find it especially beneficial when you have been on your feet all day, such as after a hard day's shopping or after a long walk.

Make the most of the time you spend soaking your feet by manicuring your nails or cleansing your face with a herbal face pack. You will then emerge looking and feeling great from top to toe.

A foot bath treatment
You will need
◇ 2oz (50g) herbs
◇ 1¹/₂pts (900ml) water
◇ Enamel or stainless steel saucepan
◇ Sieve
◇ 2tbsp sea salt

Put the herbs and water into a saucepan. Bring to the boil, then cover and simmer for 30 minutes. Strain, then stir in the sea salt. To use, add ¹/₂pt (300ml) of the decoction to a bowl of hot water. Soak your feet for 10 minutes while relaxing in a comfortable chair. Dry them well and dust with an unscented talcum powder.

Mustard bath

A mustard foot bath warms the whole body and feels particularly beneficial when you are suffering from a cold or a chill. It is also good when you have been out in very cold weather and feel frozen through; a mustard bath will thaw you out!

You will need
◇ 1tbsp black mustard seeds, crushed, or 2tsp mustard powder plus 2tbsp water
◇ ¹/₂pt (300ml) boiling water
◇ Bowl with cover

Put the crushed mustard seeds into a bowl (or work the mustard powder to a paste with the 2tbsp water). Pour on the boiling water and stir well, then cover the bowl and leave for 15 minutes. To use, add to a bowl of hot water.

▷ *Herbal foot baths relieve tired feet and revive your whole body. Relax in a comfortable chair while soaking your feet and let all your stress and tension drain out of your body through your feet.*

Herbs for foot baths	
Horsetail	Excellent for tired feet; used regularly it will reduce perspiration
Lavender	An instant tonic and refreshing
Lovage	A natural deodorant
Marjoram	Soothing
Peppermint	Tonic and refreshing; use with lovage
Sage	Soothing and healing
Thyme	Cleansing

Herb arrangements

*Deliciously aromatic and flavoursome
to use in cooking, herbs can also be made into attractive and
useful decorations. As the individual herbs in the
decoration dry, they can be used to flavour food and herbal teas
or to make beauty preparations.*

Displays of herbs make practical alternatives to floral arrangements and, as with flowers, the displays do not need to be complicated; a few bunches of fresh herbs, sitting in novelty jars on the kitchen shelf, can look just as effective as a complicated herbal wreath or swag.

For formal displays the herbs can be used fresh or dried. Fresh herbs are slightly easier to work with; the displays can then be allowed to dry, following the techniques described on pages 111-114. The herbs can be plucked from the display as needed or the display can be left intact and the subtle aroma enjoyed for many months.

Harvesting herbs

Herbs can be dried before use, but fresh material is easier to work with because it is less brittle. Always over-estimate the amount of herbs needed as herbs shrink as they dry. If picking herbs from the garden, cut them early in the day and keep in water until needed.

Choosing herbs

Create special effects for each room by varying the herbs and spices used. Culinary herbs, such as rosemary, thyme and sage, are the first choice for a kitchen display, while a combination of lavender flowers, lemon balm and scented geranium leaves would provide a refreshing, tangy scent for a bathroom display.

Combine herbs with flowers for lush-looking wreaths and other decorations. Start with flowers such as roses or lavender and add favourite herbs, plus spice pods, pine cones, seed heads or small oranges covered in cloves for extra colour and fragrance.

Flowering herbs, such as thyme, mint, hyssop and sage, are suitable for displays that are to be dried, while *Calendula* flowers and lavender spikes add colour and shape to an arrangement. More colour variation can be achieved by adding the coloured and variegated foliage of sage, mint, thyme and rue.

Keeping herbs fresh

An arrangement made solely from foliage can be kept fresh for longer by spraying daily with water. Those which contain spices should be left to dry naturally. Use the herbs as required and replace with substitute ready-wired herbs. If you plan to use the herbs when dry, let them fade naturally and simply enjoy their aroma as they dry. But do not leave herbs for too long before using them as they will become dusty and lose their essential flavour.

Drying techniques

Herb arrangements, whether used to decorate the home or given as a present, can be dried before use. Although the individual herbs shrink and curl as they lose moisture, the arrangement will keep its overall decorative shape as it gradually dries and fades.

An arrangement should, ideally, be left to dry naturally face upwards on a drying frame in a warm, well-ventilated place, away from full sunshine. Dry a few extra bunches of the foliage and flower material used for the arrangement at the same time, in case you want to make any last-minute changes or repair any mistakes. When the herbs have dried completely, sprinkle them with orris root powder and suitable essential oils to 'fix' the aroma.

If you offer a fresh herb decoration as a present and know that the recipient would eventually want to use the dried herbs, suggest that it is displayed in a warm, well-ventilated room rather than in a steamy kitchen.

Herbs as decorations

There are many appealing ways of displaying both fresh and dried herbs — from simple bunches of fresh herbs to complicated wreaths, wall-hangings, swags and garlands. Herbal arrangements make delightful gifts and they look just as effective fresh or dried. Display herbs throughout the house — not just the kitchen — as most rooms will benefit from the aroma.

▽ *Combine fragrant herbs and pretty flowers for a stunning wreath.*

Fresh kitchen herbs

Display bunches of fresh herbs, used every day, in different individual jugs and jars along a kitchen windowsill. Herbs such as parsley, rosemary and sage, look good crammed together in pots, as their foliage is very varied. When using the herbs in cooking, pluck them selectively from the jugs in order to keep the ornamental look for as long as possible.

Similarly, small mixed bunches of herbs, such as mauve chive flowers and grey sage leaves combined with the creamy-green leaves of lemon balm, make attractive and aromatic arrangements.

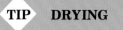

TIP	DRYING

Perennial herbs and those with small leaves and woody stems, such as thyme and rosemary, dry better than soft-stemmed herbs, such as basil. They also keep their shape well and are less likely to shrivel and crumble than soft-stemmed varieties.

Wreaths and garlands

The techniques used for making wreaths and garlands of herbs are similar to those used for the same type of floral arrangements. See pages 55-58 for information on making a wreath.

◁ *For colourful, textured effects mix flower and seed heads together.*

Dried herb baskets

Dried herbs also look appealing arranged in small wicker baskets — especially when flowering varieties are used. To make a display like this, place a block of oasis in the base of the basket and push the stems of the herbs into the oasis. Some of the herbs may need to be wired. For information on making dried flower and herb baskets, see pages 78-79.

▷ *This lovely, summer display includes bergamot, honeysuckle, borage, feverfew, rosemary and mints.*

Kitchen plait

The variety of culinary herbs used in this swag gives it great visual appeal, and all the herbs and spices could be used when cooking. A raffia plait forms the base of the swag and the herbs and spices are wired on to the plait singly or in clusters.

You will need

◇ Raffia (quantity depends on length and thickness you wish to make the plait)
◇ Small bundles of fresh herbs including spearmint, French tarragon, marjoram, parsley, curry plant, ginger mint, sage, thyme, juniper, rosemary, hyssop flowers and bay leaves
◇ Cinnamon sticks
◇ Whole bulbs of garlic
◇ Vanilla pods
◇ Red chilli peppers
  (Quantities for the above depend on size of plait)
◇ Medium gauge florists' stub wire

△ *Follow the project steps to make a decorative, yet useful, kitchen display of culinary herbs and aromatic spices.*

Making the plait

A wall-hanging needs a base that will lie flat against the wall and a plait of raffia is ideal. Raffia is available from garden centres and craft shops.

1 Bunch the raffia together until it is the thickness required for the plait. Use a small piece of raffia to tie the bunch together at one end.

2 Divide the raffia into three equal amounts and begin to plait. Work as you would if plaiting hair, winding left then right into the centre.

3 When the plait reaches the required length, secure it a few inches from the end with a second small length of raffia.

4 Make a second, narrower plait in the same way to form a generous loop for hanging the swag. Cut the ends to an even length. Twist into a loop (as shown in diagram) and attach to the main plait, using wire.

Decorating the plait

Decide how the finished plait should look before adding the herbs and spices. Experiment by grouping them along the length of the plait. A simple linear pattern should be worked from top to bottom; but, for a central focal point, start in the middle and work outwards towards each end of the plait.

1 Wire each type of herb into a bundle of three to four stems, leaving a long piece of wire. Push this through the front of the plait and flatten it against the back. Cut off any excess wire.

2 Place the next bunch of herbs to overlap the first and wire on to the plait in the same way. Continue working in this way along the length of the plait.

3 Once all the herbs have been added, start embellishing the plait with extras, such as bulbs of garlic, chilli peppers, nutmeg, cinnamon sticks and vanilla pods. Wire the pods and garlic so that you can fix them by their stems on to the plait. Wrap wire round the middle of a bundle of two or three cinnamon sticks and around the nutmeg.

4 Once you have finished decorating the plait, hang it from a hook on a kitchen dresser, a cupboard door or on a wall.

△ *For a formal wreath to celebrate successful exam results use bay leaves — the herb traditionally associated with academic awards.*

CHAPTER V

CRAFTED FROM NATURE

◇

Corn dollies

*Making a corn dolly at harvest time is a
custom dating right back to the roots of history. Ever since
crops have been grown, agricultural communities all
over the world have created decorative straw objects which play
a central role in harvest and fertility rites.*

A corn dolly is defined as an abstract shape incorporating the grain of the crop used in its making. There are hundreds of different designs, originating not only from the rural communities of Britain but also from around the world. New designs are still being created and the art of decorative straw work, which incorporates corn dollies, is enjoying a significant growth in popularity.

The decorated wooden spoon featured in this section is a beginner's project, using just a few simple plaits and shapes. More experienced workers may wish to substitute more complicated plaits. For example, lengths of plaits can themselves be plaited together and then used to decorate the spoon. The way the straws are folded across the plait can also be varied to give different effects. For a more colourful finish, the spoon can be painted, stained or varnished before the trimmings are added.

Decorative ribbons

The ribbons used to decorate corn dollies are part of the harvest and fertility traditions. Different colours are symbolically used in straw work to depict varying themes: red is for the poppy in the field and the sun; blue embodies both the corn-flower in the field and water; green represents the new growth during spring; gold symbolizes the grain of the crop and the goddess; and white depicts purity.

Materials and equipment

In addition to the following items you will need a peg or clip, to hold the work if you have to stop mid-plait, and a tape measure, to check the length of the plaits.

Straw

Wheat, oats, rye and barley are all used to make corn dollies and come under the general heading of 'straw'. Wheat is the easiest, most versatile type to use, while barley is rather fragile to work with.

When buying straw, check what type it is. The straw used for this project is one of the old varieties, called Maris Widgeon, specially grown by farmers for straw work. It grows up to six feet tall and has hollow, thin-walled stems. Modern types are not as suitable as they are shorter and have pithy stems.

The straw has to be harvested by hand or binder. Any that has been through a combine harvester is useless for straw work as the machinery chews up the stems. Straw is normally purchased direct from the farm at harvest time. Some suppliers do keep stocks all year. They can also supply ready prepared straw and may even send sheaves through the post.

Sorting the straw The straw must be prepared into working lengths. The section normally used is the top part, from the ear to the first leaf joint. When purchasing straw, check that the top section has an average length of at least 12in (30cm).

Prepare the straw, then grade it into bundles of the different thicknesses and store it in a dry, airy container until needed. For easy reference, the thinner end of the

Decorating a wooden spoon

This is a simple project, suitable for absolute beginners, but easily adapted to suit different levels of skill. The three strand 'hair' plait used for this project is the most simple and versatile of all straw plaits and can be made with varying numbers of straws.

Apart from being a pretty kitchen ornament, this straw work spoon would also make an ideal wedding day keepsake or gift.

You will need

◇ Wooden spoon: overall length approximately 14in (36cm); handle length 9.5in (24cm)
◇ 12 thick straws with matching heads, 14in (36cm) long
  ◇ 3 medium straws with matching heads, 17in (43cm) long
  ◇ 3 fine straws with matching heads, 12in (30cm) long
  ◇ All-purpose adhesive
  ◇ Dried flowers and grasses
  ◇ Thread
  ◇ White ribbon

1 Using thread, tie the three medium straws together just below the heads. Make a simple three strand plait, measuring 13in (33cm) long. Tie off the ends with thread. (The aim is to produce an even plait with a straight edge to wind along the handle of the spoon.)

straw, below the ear, is called the tip, the thicker end, by the leaf joint, is called the butt.

Thread
Use a strong, straw-coloured thread. The thickness of the thread varies according to the project being undertaken: use cotton-covered polyester thread for delicate work and crochet cotton (grade 10) or linen thread for heavier work.

Scissors
Use small needlework scissors with points. If you intend to do a lot of straw work, put aside a pair specifically for this work, as the straw will blunt the blades.

Trough
Soak the straw, prior to working it, by laying it flat in some water. Use a plant trough of suitable length or a wallpaper tray; alternatively, use the bath or a large sink. Do not bend the straw in order to make it fit the container, as this will damage the stems. Only soak as much straw as required.

Towels
Towels are important both for protecting the work surface from scratches and for keeping the straw covered and damp before use. Do not leave straw wrapped in a damp towel when not in use — it will either go mouldy or, as it is still growing, it may start to sprout!

Preparing the straw
Soak as many pieces of straw as are needed by laying them in the trough and covering them with lukewarm water. Weight the straw down to stop it floating. The duration of soaking varies according to the variety, thickness and age of the straw — normally allow twenty to thirty minutes. It is ready when the butt end can be bent without it cracking — when ready, remove it and wrap it in a towel.

Tying the knot
A clove hitch knot or a surgeon's knot are the two most suitable for straw work since they can be tightened to grip the straw before the final granny knot is made.

2 The heart is made from two plaits, each 5in (12.5cm) long. Use six straws to make each plait and work the plait as before, this time grouping two straws together for each strand. To produce the pattern of the plait, the straws should not cross or lay on top of each other: to achieve this, move the inside straw of each group first so that the straws lay side by side in the plait.

3 Secure ends with thread; join the two plaits together at right angles across original ties at tip ends. Fasten the plaits to the wooden spoon at the point where the bowl joins the handle.

4 Bend plaits to form a heart shape; attach to spoon by tying across ties at butt end of plaits, 2in (5cm) further up handle.

5 Fasten the long, straight ends of straw to the back of the spoon. Trim to neaten.

6 Add the plait made from the three medium straws. Tie or

glue the tip end of the plait to the back of the spoon, positioning it level with the top part of the heart. Wind it over the butt end ties to conceal them and up the handle. Secure 2½in (6cm) from top of handle. Remove the heads.

7 Make the lover's knot to decorate the top of the spoon handle by plaiting the three fine straws together. The plait should be 6in (15cm) long. Secure the ends and then twist the plait into a lover's knot. Tie the tip and butt ends together.

8 Tie the completed lover's knot to the top of the handle, making sure that it covers the end of the plait wound up the spoon. Leave the thread ends long to make a loop for hanging the finished spoon from a hook or nail.

9 Arrange the ears of wheat so that they spread out attractively. Allow the plaits to dry. Finish off with ribbon bows; then decorate with dried flowers and grasses secured in place with all-purpose adhesive.

DESIGN IDEAS

Once you have mastered some of the basic straw work techniques, you can go on to create a wide variety of items, from decorative wall hangings to delicate jewellery.

TIP	FINISHING

If you need to rearrange the ears of wheat in a design, they must first be dampened slightly. Move the ribbons out of the way and put a warm, damp cloth over the ears for ten minutes. The ears should then be flexible enough for any adjustments to be made. Allow them to dry, keeping the ears of wheat in the correct position.

▽ *This striking ring of wheat is based on a simple, three strand hair plait. Its impressive look is achieved by using a large number of straws in each group of the plait, with a new bunch of straws fed in to each right hand movement of the plaiting to give extra width.*

△ *Here, fine straw plaits have been twisted into lover's knots, then glued to jewellery attachments to make dainty earrings.*

▷ *This harvest braid, crowned with a lover's knot, has been made from barley, which, although difficult to work with, gives a lovely effect.*

Basketry 1

*Once the basic techniques of basketry have been
mastered, you can go on to create both functional and attractive
items for the home and garden. A whole range
of plant materials, along with a variety of techniques, can be used
to produce beautiful basketware.*

Today basketry is valued for its decorative merit, but in the past it was given much greater significance. Among North American Indians, the ability to make a beautiful basket was the most important virtue a woman could possess. In ancient times basketry was an essential part of mythology and ritual, with the patterns given symbolic meanings. Baskets were buried with the dead to help them in their afterlife.

Basketry has changed little over the centuries as skills were handed down from one generation to the next. Although the plants, techniques and shapes used for hundreds of years are still popular, the craft adapts well to modern materials. Surprisingly beautiful items are now made of woven plastic and even from cardboard.

Once the basic techniques of basketry have been mastered, discover the joy of creating useful, everyday items. Experiment to find ways of expressing your own style. On pages 129-132 we will go on to explain how to apply the basic techniques covered here.

Types of raw material

Before you start learning the techniques involved in basketry, it is important to discover the range of natural material that is available. You will find that they may help to inspire your projects. Basketry materials can be bought from some garden centres and craft shops.

In temperate climates, rush and willow were once the only options for basketry. Today, there are some imported materials that provide exotic alternatives: cane and bamboo from the tropics; grass from the plains; and bark, twigs and split wood from forest regions.

Willow, grown commercially for basketry, is mainly of the variety *Salix triandra* ('Black Mauls'), although other types are also used. All are sold in bundles according to the colour and length of rods, which range from 3-8ft (90-240cm) long.

Cane, or rattan, comes from the climbing palms, *Calumnus* and *Daemonorops*. Cane is sold in 7-30ft (2-9m) lengths of narrow, round or flat sections. It is graded from 00 for the finest stems to 20 for the thickest. Although cane varies in price, cheaper types are often of the same quality as costly ones.

Rush mainly comes from the stems of club rush or true bulrush (*Scirpus lacustris*). Occasionally, soft rush (*Juncus effusus*) is also used. Rush is sold in lengths of up to 10ft (3m), in bundles of mixed thicknesses.

Raffia comes from the leaf undersides of the palm *Raffia ruffia*. These are dried and split into several widths. The split sections are then made into small bundles for selling.
Coppiced wood comes from a variety of trees. Traditional sources include Sweet or Spanish chestnut (*Castanea sativa*), hazel (*Corylus avellana*) and ash (*Fraxinus excelsior*). Whole or split stems are available for making large, strong baskets, as well as for making frames, handles or reinforcing smaller baskets. Use finely split stems for delicate, intricate work.

Other materials

Cereal crops, including wheat, barley, oat and rye straw, with the ears and leaves removed, are used to make baskets and hats. Baskets made from tropical woven vines have attractively irregular shapes.

Various palm leaves, especially the date palm (*Phoenix dactylifera*) and screw palm (*Pandanus spp.*), are

▽ *Once you have mastered the basics of basketry, enjoy creating your own designs. Plain patterns, with only a little detail, can be as striking in their simplicity as more ornate, decorative designs.*

popular for the tropical-style basketry, such as sun hats and plant holders, often seen in tourist souvenir shops. Split bamboo is a favourite oriental material that is popular for making screens.

You can even grow and dry your own plant materials for basketry. Iris, gladioli, red-hot poker, crocosmia, maize and yucca foliage, as well as spruce, cedar, heather and alder roots can all be made into baskets.

Tools and equipment

Early basket makers had only their teeth and sharp stones or bones for use as primitive tools. Nowadays you will find the following items are available; some you may already have.

Secateurs should be of the double-blade, 'parrot-beak' type. The single-blade, anvil types can crush and spoil the material.

Craft knives are best bought with angled ends and replaceable blades, or blades that can be sharpened.

Side cutters are plier-shaped cutting tools; one with a pointed nose is best. Alternatively, use wire cutters.

Bodkins are mild steel tools with wooden handles; they come in many sizes. Options are a metal knitting needle or metal skewer.

A flexible steel tape measure is needed for measuring straight or curved lengths.

Screwblocks are two pieces of wood bolted together. They are used to hold stakes rigid while you make a rectangular or square base. You could use a vice, or two pieces of wood and 'G-clamps' instead.

Weights are needed to hold baskets steady while they are being built up. Use round metal weights, large stones or plastic-wrapped bricks.

A large sink or trough is necessary for soaking the materials before use, but a bath will do.

Rapping irons are used to compress and level willow work; they are heavy iron rectangles about 20-25cm (8-10in) long. You could use a small hammer instead.

Picking knives have a sharp, curved blade and are mainly used for trimming willow work.

Commanders are used to help straighten willow rods. A commander is a metal rod with either a ring at each end or a ring at one end and a hook at the other.

Round-nosed pliers are used to squeeze canes so that they can bend without cracking.

side cutters

round-nosed pliers

secateurs

craft knife

picking knife

rapping iron

bodkin

steel tape measure

raffia

coppiced wood

cane rush willow

weight

Basic techniques

Inflexible materials such as willow and cane must be soaked in hot water before use so that they can be bent without cracking.

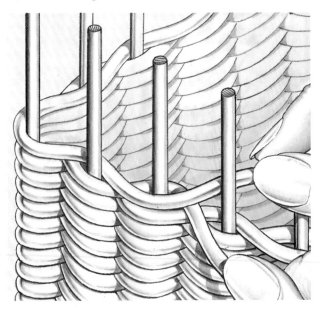

Stake and strand basketry has a rigid frame of spaced-out uprights (stakes) which form the sides, either radiating around the base of round baskets or standing straight on square baskets. Two flexible weavers (the strands running across the basket) are tightly interwoven from the base upwards. Willow and cane are the most common materials for this basketry technique but other woods and rush are also used.

Use grasses, rushes, roots or bark fibre to create decorative geometric patterns, or weave in ornamental materials, such as feathers. To add these materials, twist two weavers around the upright stakes. This produces baskets that are flexible but strong.

Coiling is an easy, but time consuming, technique that lends itself to colourful, geometric patterns. A core is formed from grasses, rushes, straw or rope. This is wrapped with raffia, chair cane, wild clematis, twine, string, fine split wood or even young bramble shoots. The core may show through or be covered. The wrapped core is formed into concentric circles which are sewn together with split cane or raffia.

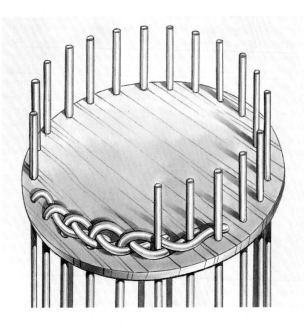

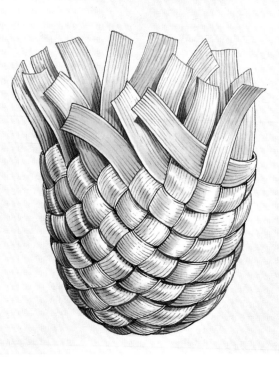

Hard-based basketry is built on a strong wooden base with holes drilled around the edge. Willow or cane is used for both the stakes and the woven infill of the basket. The stakes are added through holes in the base and woven together underneath.

Plaiting involves the interlacing of three or more strands. It calls for long, flat strips of similar width and thickness. Rush, cane, bamboo, bark, split wood and reeds are all ideal for plaiting. The finished work can be rigid or soft, with the plait used flat or on an edge. Edges are left unsewn or coiled and sewn together.

Basketry 2

The techniques for weaving using the stake and strand method are as varied as the shapes that can be created. From a humble table mat to an intricately patterned linen basket, the theory is the same; it is how you choose to combine the weaves that makes each project unique.

Stake and strand basketry is a classic form which takes its name from the upright spokes of the basket (the stakes) and the horizontal weavers (the strands). Usually the stakes are quite thick, providing the framework and strength, while the strands are finer and more flexible, giving stability and surface interest to the basket.

Materials

Willow and cane are the traditional materials for stake and strand weaving, but a similar material, such as bamboo, could be used instead.

Willow

Part of the beauty of weaving with willow is the variation in thickness down its length. The base is the widest part and is known as the butt; this tapers to the tip. Willows by their nature are not straight, and their curved shape can be used to advantage during weaving.

Individual lengths of willow are known as rods. They are sold in bundles called bolts, which vary in length from 3-8ft (1-2.5m).

Willow is available in three natural colours: brown, buff and white; brown being the cheapest and white the most expensive. It is possible to dye willow, but this is not an easy process.

Cane

Cane is available from Very Very Fine 000 size to No.20, which is ⁵⁄₁₆in (8mm) wide. It varies in quality too, with Continental Green Label and Blue Tie being the best, and Bleached being the weakest. Far Eastern Red Tie is a good compromise for most purposes.

Because cane is very absorbent, it is easy to dye. This makes it popular for brightly coloured baskets, where the colours are mixed in the weave to form different patterns.

Storage and preparation
Willow

Keep willow in a dark, dry, cool and well-ventilated place until you are ready to use it. This is important, because the quality of the willow will be impaired if it is not stored in the right conditions.

To make the rods flexible before use, immerse them in water for two hours, then lie them flat under a damp towel and leave overnight. Keep the willow covered while you work as it dries out quickly. After two days, dry out unused rods and re-soak, otherwise they will go mouldy. Dry left-over rods thoroughly and store for future use.

Cane

Cane requires the same conditions as willow for storage. Do not store cane coiled up, as it will adopt the shape and end up looking like a huge spring.

To prepare cane for weaving, place it in very hot water for a few minutes so that it will bend in weaving without cracking. Do not soak for long periods as the cane will discolour. Dry out spare cane thoroughly as damp cane attracts mould which will leave tell-tale black speckles.

Basic weaves

There is a huge variety of weaves from which to choose. They fall into three categories: randing, pairing and waling. The following are the basic weaves of each type.

Randing

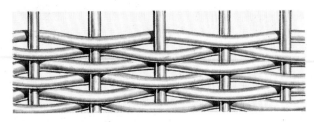

This is a very simple form of weaving, where a single strand is worked alternately in front of and behind an odd number of stakes.

There are variations on the basic randing technique which produce different effects.

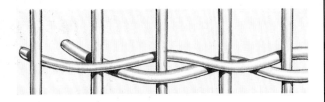

Follow-on randing is worked when there is an even number of stakes. A strand is woven in and out of the stakes as for basic randing, with another strand starting in the space behind the first and worked over and under the stakes, in the opposite way to the first. Keep the first strand ahead of the second at all times.

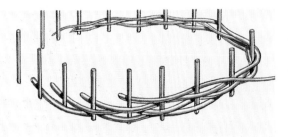

English randing is perfectly suited to willow, as the tapering nature of the rods forms an diagonal line on the basket. Choose rods of a regular length and thickness, and there should be as many rods as there are stakes. Starting with the butt end, the first rod is worked in the basic randing method to its tip. The second rod is started in the next space to the right of the first, again butt end first. The weave continues in this way until a level edge is formed.

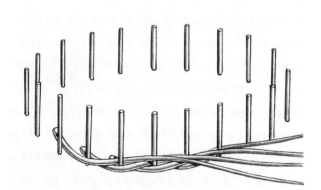

French randing also requires as many evenly sized rods as there are stakes. But, unlike English randing, all the rods are worked at the same time. The first rod is started with the butt end over and under two stakes. The second rod is started in the same way, from the next space to the left of the first. All the rods are started in this way until every space is filled. Then a second row is worked by weaving over and under the next two stakes.

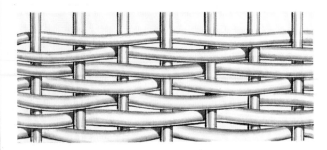

Rib randing creates a diagonal design, or vertical stripes if three different coloured rods are used. When the number of stakes is not divisible by three, form the weave by taking the strand over two stakes and under one, all the way around the basket. When the number of stakes is divisible by three, use three strands in the follow-on method of randing (left), following the over-two-under-one pattern.

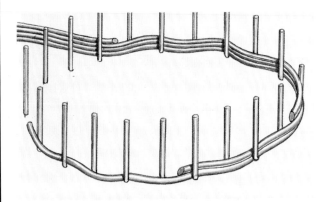

Slewing is simply randing with more than one strand, where two to five rods are woven together as if they were one. An odd number of stakes are needed. Rand one rod from butt end to about a third of its length, then add in the butt of another rod and rand them together for another third. Add another butt and work the three rods together. When the first rod ends, insert the butt of another rod at the top.

Pairing

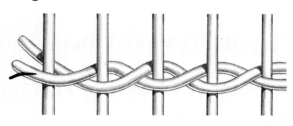

A pair of weavers are worked together to form this strong weave, which is traditionally used for basket bases. The two weavers are started in adjacent spaces, and are then taken over and under one another, whilst alternating in front of and behind the stakes.

Waling

This forms a rope-like weave which is used at the edge of bases to provide a ledge for the basket to sit on, and to prepare the rods for the border. It is worked with three to six rods, in a similar way to pairing. Each strand is taken over one less stake than the number of weavers, before going behind a stake. Each strand is worked in turn in this way.

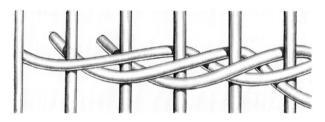

Three-rod waling is worked with three strands starting in adjacent spaces. If using willow, put the narrow tips into the stakes. Begin waling by taking the left-hand weaver over two stakes and under one, bringing the rod back to the front in line with its starting position. Work the other two rods in the same way.

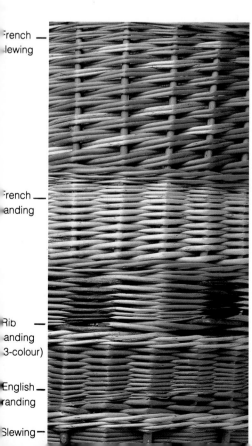

French slewing

French randing

Rib randing (3-colour)

English randing

Slewing

Follow-on slewing and French slewing are working using the same principles as follow-on randing and French randing, but two or more rods are used together and woven as one.

Table mats

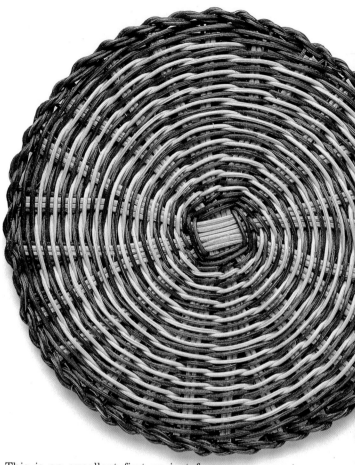

This is an excellent first project for a newcomer to basketry, as it covers the basic techniques without the need for complicated shaping. Do not underestimate the value of practising on table mats, as the methods used here are the same as those used to make the bases of most baskets. The finished cane mats measure 9¾in (25cm). This mat is made with natural and black cane, which are alternately woven together around the mat. The edging is formed by twisting black stakes to form a decorative rope border.

You will need

◇ 12 base sticks 10⅝in (27cm) long of No.8 (3mm) natural cane
◇ 24 sticks 4⅜in (11cm) long of No.8 (3mm) natural cane
◇ 52 border stakes 6¾in (17cm) long of No.5 (2.5mm) black cane
◇ Weavers of No.5 (2.5mm) in black and natural cane
◇ Side cutters
◇ Bodkin

1 Using the bodkin, pierce the centre of six of the base sticks and thread the other six through. This is called the slath.

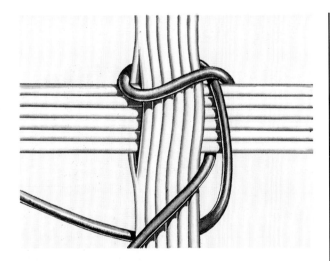

2 Take a black No.5 (2.5mm) cane and form a loop over one of the slaths. Take one end over the next arm, and the other end under it. Then swap, taking the one that went under the arm last time over the next arm, and visa-versa. This is known as tying in the slath with pairing. Work around the slath for two complete rows in this way.

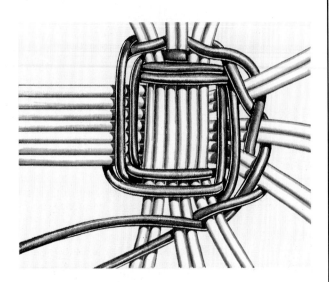

3 For the third row, separate each arm of six sticks into three pairs, for form 12 slaths with two sticks in each and continue pairing.

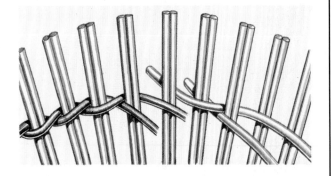

4 On the fourth row, add two natural No.5 (2.5mm) weavers in the two spaces immediately to the right of the black weavers, as shown. Continue pairing for fourteen rows, using the two colours and keeping the natural cane ahead of the black cane all the time. Leave the weavers.

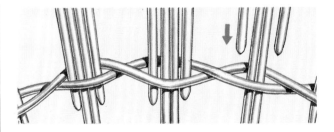

5 Extra sticks have to be added at this stage so that the mat fans out to take its circular shape. Cut a point at one end of each of the 4⅜in (11cm) long sticks (there are 24) and insert them one either side of each pair of sticks.

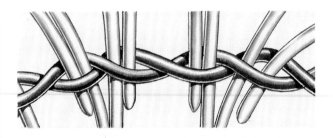

6 Continue pairing, separating the sticks into pairs as you go along, to weave in the new sticks, for 24 rows in total. Cut the natural coloured pair of weavers at the wrong side and work one more row with the black pair.

To work rope border

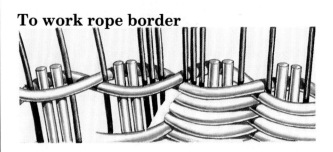

1 Cut a point on one end of each of the 52 border stakes and insert 48 of them, each one either side of the pairs of natural sticks. Insert two of the spare border stakes next to one of the border stakes you have just added. Insert the extra two stakes beside the adjacent border stake. Trim the natural sticks.

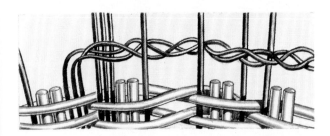

2 Twist the first bunch of three border stakes away from you and bring in front of the next and then behind. On the third bunch start picking up the two longest ends at back to make three with the border stake. Twist each bunch away from you the same number of times and keep weaving until edge is finished. Trim ends at back.

Fashionable feathers

*Create your own style with jewellery and
hair accessories made from a kaleidoscope of coloured feathers.
Set off with fake gemstones to form elegant earrings,
or combined in rich shades to decorate a hair comb,
they add individuality to any outfit.*

From the ostrich feather fans of the ancient Egyptians to the elegant hat trimmings of the Victorian lady, feathers have always held their place in high fashion. Dyed and trimmed to perfection they shone as bright as jewels in the hair and on the clothing of stylish women.

Today, with the demise of the hat and the extinction of the fan, and awareness about endangered bird species, large feathers are rarely used as dress accessories, yet the small brilliantly coloured plumes, available from haberdashers and craft shops, make an inexpensive and attractive alternative to modern costume jewellery.

Feather accessories

Feathers are available in a wide range of natural and brilliantly dyed colours. Their decorative possibilities are endless — hats, belts and bags can all be given a personal touch with the addition of a few well-placed plumes, and jewellery can be created in exotic shapes and forms.

Just gather together a selection of coloured feathers with matching fake gemstones and experiment with various combinations until you find the ones you like best. Then simply fix them to your mounts with a strong solvent adhesive (tweezers are useful for manipulating the feathers into place).

You can choose colours to match your outfits, or mix vibrant shades for a party feel. For a more casual look, select natural undyed feathers and wear them with denim to create a western effect.

You will need
◇ Feathers
◇ Hair comb
◇ Hair clip
◇ Clip-on earring backs (for earrings and shoe clips) or earring fittings for pierced ears
◇ Fine grade sandpaper
◇ Solvent adhesive
◇ Fake gemstones
◇ Sequins or beads
◇ Tweezers

Making earrings and shoe clips

Apply a small amount of glue to the front of the clip and place the large plain feathers in position. If the front of your clip is particularly small, cut a circular piece of card 1in (2.5cm) in diameter and stick this to the clip. This will provide a better base for the feathers. Apply a second layer of glue and then stick the smaller feathers in place, followed by the gemstone. Then arrange a circle of sequins or beads to frame your gemstone and put aside to dry before use.

Decorating a hair comb or clip

1 Sand a small portion of the plastic along the top of the comb or clip with fine grade sandpaper so that the glue gets a good fix.

2 Apply a small amount of glue to the sanded section and stick the large feathers in position using the tweezers.

3 Apply a second layer of glue and lay the smaller feathers, the fake gemstone and then the sequins or beads in place. Put aside to dry before use.

Simple woodwork

*Inspired by the art deco designs of the 1930s,
this wooden furniture is simple and quick to make. The tray,
coffee table and mirror will brighten up any room,
especially with a bold paint effect. For a softer finish, use
the warm natural tones of the wood itself.*

Wood is a remarkable material. It is a versatile, strong, cheap and renewable resource which requires little pre-treatment before it can be used. These qualities have made it a popular choice for all kinds of different applications, from the humble wooden spoon to beautifully carved musical instruments.

Although there is a huge variety of tree species, the timber itself falls into just two categories: softwood and hardwood. Softwood trees are almost all cone-bearing and, with the exception of larch, have evergreen needles. In contrast, hardwood trees have broad leaves and populate the forests of the world – notably the dwindling rainforests of South America.

Wood is warm to the touch, soft on the eye and flexible in the hands of a craftsman, with enough variety of colour to suit any design requirement. This is why both types of timber have been used throughout history as the raw material for furniture making – from the simplicity of the Shaker style to the carved intricacy of Chippendale.

The best way to learn woodworking techniques is to begin with simple pieces of furniture, such as the smart trio illustrated on these pages. The tray is the best project to begin with; the coffee table and mirror complete the set. These are all easy enough for a novice with no previous woodworking experience to attempt. Success will depend simply upon accuracy and precision during construction.

Materials and equipment

Timber

Softwood is ideal for this furniture. Ask for PAR (planed all round) wood, which has had all its sides smoothed – it will therefore be slightly smaller on all sides than the size you ask for, so order accordingly. Ask the merchant to cut the timber to the exact length required, to leave you with one less job to do at home.

Paint or stain

Oil-based paint If you want a flat colour finish that hides the wood grain, use an oil-based paint. It is hard-wearing and there is a huge range of colours available, but the wood will need careful preparation before the final coat is applied.

Knots should be painted with knotting to prevent them from bleeding through the paint. A coat of primer and at least one undercoat

---

Tray

This simple tray makes a perfect accompaniment to the coffee table. Its dimensions are 23½ x 14in (60 x 35cm), which is large enough to carry a snack meal or tea for two.

You will need
◇ One piece softwood 1in (2.5cm) thick by 14in (35cm) wide by 23½in (60cm) long for the base
◇ Six softwood battens 1in (2.5cm) square by 14in (35cm) long for the ends and feet
◇ Two chrome steel tubes ⁵⁄₁₆in (8mm) diameter by 23½in (60cm) long for the side rails
◇ Nails, 1½in (4cm) ovals
◇ Fine glass paper
◇ Paint or stain in chosen colours
◇ 1in (2.5cm) paint brush
◇ Drill and ³⁄₃₂in (2mm) bit and ⁵⁄₁₆in (8mm) spade bit
◇ PVA woodworking adhesive (wood glue)
◇ Hammer

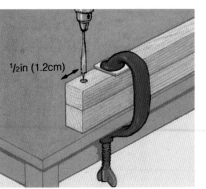

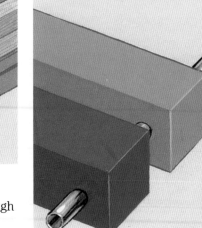

1 Lightly sand the ends of all timber lengths to remove rough edges. Lay two batten lengths exactly one on top of the other; hold securely (preferably with a cramp). Mark a point ½in (1.2cm) from one end for the hole to slot the chrome tube through. Using the ⁵⁄₁₆in (8mm) bit, drill through both battens. Repeat at the opposite end. Use one of these battens as a template to mark identical positions on two more battens. Drill in the same way.

2 Paint or stain all the timber lengths as desired. When dry, insert the chrome tubes through holes in the battens, extending them ⁵⁄₈in (1.5cm) out beyond the outer battens. Place on the work top and measure a ½in (1.2cm) space between battens. Check that all measurements are accurate.

Table

This 55 x 19in table is both screwed and glued together.

You will need
◇ Three softwood planks 1in (2.5cm) thick by 55in (140cm) long by 6in (15cm) wide, for the table top
◇ Two pieces softwood 1in (2.5cm) thick by 19in (47.5cm) long by 8in (20cm) wide for the legs
◇ Twelve softwood battens 1in (2.5cm) square by 19in (47.5cm)
◇ Fine glass paper
◇ Paint or stain in chosen colours
◇ 1in (2.5cm) paint brush
◇ No 8, 1½in (3.8cm) counter-sunk screws
◇ Drill and ⅕in (5mm) drill bit
◇ PVA woodworking adhesive (wood glue)
◇ Screwdriver

1 Lightly sand ends of all timber lengths to remove rough edges. Paint or stain all sections.

2 On four of the battens mark three points centrally along one side, 2in (5cm) from each end with the third centred between the outer two. Drill holes through the battens at these points to make fixing points to the table top.

3 On two drilled battens turn to the adjacent side and mark two holes 2¾in (7cm) from each end and drill for attaching battens to leg. Mark these as battens A.

4 On the two other drilled battens mark two positions 1½in (3.8cm) from each end; drill holes through battens at these points to make fixing points into battens A. Mark these two as B.

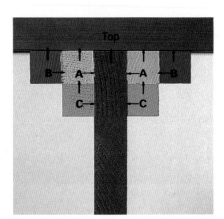

5 Take two more battens; mark, then drill, 1½in (4cm) from each end and at a centre point between the two. These fix the battens to the leg. Turn to the adjacent side; mark, then drill 3¼in (8cm) from each end to join the battens to A. Mark these as C.

is necessary before the final coat is applied, which can be a satin or gloss finish. Sand lightly before applying each coat of paint.

Staining A coloured wood finish which allows the grain of the wood to show through would also be suitable. Some contain both stain and protective finish in one and are applied with a cloth. Two coats are recommended. Gloss and satin finishes are both available.

Other finishes You could also use an opaque or semi-translucent, coloured finish. These are brushed on and provide a protective satin finish. If a matt or gloss finish is required, clear varnish can be used.

Testers of some products are available to enable you to check the colour before making a final choice.

Adhesive

Where required, use a PVA wood-working adhesive (wood glue) designed for this type of work. Carefully follow the instructions that come with it.

Nails or screws

Both nails and screws are required. The wood into which the head end of the nail or screw goes needs to be drilled to allow the head to sit comfortably in the wood.

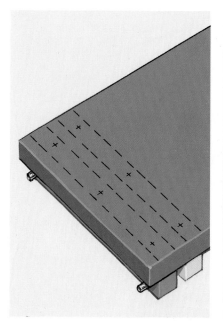

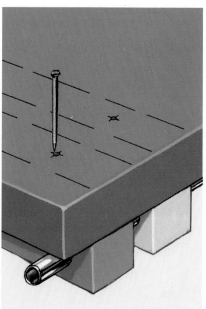

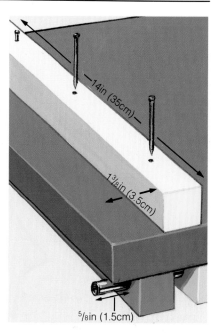

3 Place tray base on top of battens. Mark positions along the width of the tray for three nails to go through the base into each batten.

4 Remove top section and, with ³/₃₂in (2mm) bit, drill holes through base in marked positions. Glue battens to base and secure with nails through the holes.

5 Mark and drill three holes in each leg batten as above. Glue and nail to underside of tray, centring each leg below pairs of battens, 1³/₈in (3.5cm) from end.

6 Following the method described in the previous step, repeat this with all the remaining battens.

7 Place an A batten to each side of a leg; glue then screw down. Put planks top side down – ½in (1.2cm) space between each. Place leg 10in (25cm) from one end and clamp. Glue and screw A battens to planks.

8 Glue and screw B pieces to A pieces then to the top. Glue and screw Cs to the leg, and to As.

9 Using the same technique, attach the other leg to the main body of the table.

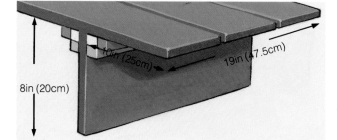

TIP	SECURING WOOD

◇ Tap a nail in gently at first, then grip the hammer near to the end and with your wrist rigid, strike the nail head with a clean stroke from the elbow.

◇ Flatten the point of a nail with a hammer before putting in close to the end of a piece of wood. This helps stop the wood splitting.

◇ Wipe away any excess glue immediately with a cloth and warm water.

◇ Don't overdo the amount of glue; you only need a thin strip down the centre of each batten.

◇ To avoid bruising the wood with the hammer, drive the nail almost home then use a nail punch for the final part. A wire nail makes a good nail punch if you blunt the point first.

Mirror

This free-standing mirror can be used to complement the coffee table and tray, or to brighten up a bedroom or bathroom.

You will need
◇ Mirror ⅕in (5mm) thick, and 20in (50cm) by 12in (30cm) with bevelled edges
◇ Ply backing same size as mirror and adhesive
◇ Timber 1in (2.5cm) thick, 12in (30cm) x 6⅕in (15.5cm) for base
◇ Four battens 12in (30cm) long by 1in (2.5cm) square
◇ Six 1in (2.5cm) cubes of timber
◇ Ply offcuts
◇ Nails, 1½in (3.8cm) ovals
◇ Fine glass paper
◇ Paint or stain in chosen colours
◇ 1in (2.5cm) paint brush
◇ Drill and ³⁄₃₂in (2mm) drill bit
◇ PVA woodworking adhesive (wood glue)
◇ Hammer

1 Lightly sand ends of all timber lengths to remove rough edges. Paint or stain all sections as shown (sides of base have been painted to look like attached battens). Using mirror adhesive fix the mirror to the ply backing.

2 When paint is dry place two battens side by side. Drill, glue and nail them together. Repeat with the other two battens. Position the two sets of battens on timber base, allowing a central slot for the mirror, (see picture on right). Mark positions for nails on underside of each end of base to secure battens. Drill holes at marked points. Glue and nail the four battens in place from underside of the base.

3 Turn the base over, place the mirror in the slot, and glue one 1in (2.5cm) timber cube to each end of each side of mirror slot, making sure all batten ends are flush.

4 Glue two ply offcuts 1in (2.5cm) by ½in (1.2cm) together so that they form one piece, ¼in (6mm) thick. Then glue the last two 1in (2.5cm) cubes to either side of this so that a notch is formed in the centre for the mirror. Touch up the ply with matching paint. When dry attach as the top

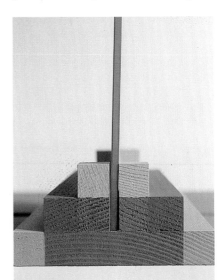

Plant stand

*Display a range of pot plants on this
attractive, tiered plant stand made from timber. The stand
has three tiers of graduating sizes and it is
designed to be placed against a wall. The timber can be left
natural, or stained a strong colour.*

This elegant, yet very practical, tiered plant stand is fairly easy to construct with the aid of wooden dowels. When finished, the plant stand measures approximately 31½in (80cm) high and 39½in (100cm) wide.

You will need

◇ Three pieces of softwood 39½in (100cm) long by 8in (20cm) wide by 1¼in (3.2cm) thick, for the side and centre uprights
◇ Two pieces of softwood 29½in (75cm) long by 9½in (24cm) wide by 1¼in (3.2cm) thick, for the bottom shelf
◇ Two pieces of softwood 19½in (49.5cm) long by 9½in (24cm) wide by 1¼in (3.2cm) thick, for the middle shelf
◇ One piece of softwood 17¾in (45cm) long by 9½in (24cm) wide by 1¼in (3.2cm) thick, to make the top shelf
◇ At least fourteen ⅓in (8mm) diameter dowels
◇ Drill
◇ Wood glue
◇ Twelve No.6 by ¾in (2cm) long screws
◇ Screwdriver
◇ Tracing paper
◇ Carbon paper
◇ Graph paper, with 1½in (4cm) square scale
◇ Sandpaper
◇ Coping saw or jig saw
◇ A few long nails
◇ Dark green water-based or acrylic paint depending on use
◇ Paint brush
◇ Polyurethane varnish

Preparation

Enlarge the scale diagrams using graph paper, taking care to copy all the positioning marks and dotted lines. Then, by using carbon paper or by going over the outlines with a sharp pencil, transfer the diagrams on to the wood as follows:

1 Mark the top shelf template on to the $17^3/4$in (45cm) long piece of wood.

2 Mark middle shelf template twice (once right side up and once reverse side up) on to the $19^1/2$in (49.5cm) long piece of wood.

3 Mark bottom shelf part (with dotted line against the long side of the wood) twice (as with the middle shelf) on to the $29^1/2$in (75cm) long piece of wood.

4 Mark side upright twice on to two of the three $39^1/2$in (100cm) long pieces of wood and the middle upright on the remaining $39^1/2$in (100cm) long piece of wood.

5 Mark the semi-circular bottom shelf templates on to the remaining pieces of wood.

6 Using the coping saw or jig saw, cut out all sections. Saw side notches at ends of middle and bottom shelves at a slight angle, as side uprights are attached at an angle. Smooth all the rough edges using sandpaper.

Assembling the shelves

1 Mark the position of dowels on top shelf with a pencil — places are marked with a cross on template. The dowels for the top shelf are fixed underneath the shelf, with the four dowels on the straight side positioned $5/8$in (1.5cm) away from straight edge.

2 With the marks as a guide, and using the hand drill and a $3/8$in (9mm) high speed drill bit, drill a hole $3/4$in (2cm) deep for each dowel — do not drill all the way through the wood.

3 Place head end of nails into holes, leaving points sticking out slightly. Push the top shelf against the upright to which it needs to be attached. The imprint made by the nails marks the positions of holes to be drilled in upright. Repeat for all uprights.

4 Remove the nails. Put wood glue into holes in top shelf; insert a dowel into each hole. Put glue in corresponding holes on centre upright; join the two parts together. Leave them to dry.

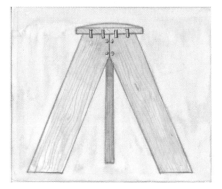

5 Glue together two side uprights where they meet at top. Glue holes in top of side uprights and join to top shelf, as before. Leave to dry. Using $3/4$in (2cm) screws, secure uprights at back (see diagram for positioning).

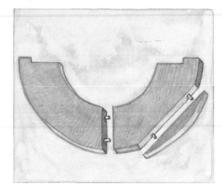

6 Join two middle shelf sections using wood glue and dowels. Attach the small semicircles of wood to main sections of bottom shelf using dowels. Join together bottom shelf sections with dowels.

7 Thoroughly sandpaper the joins between sections of wood.

8 Insert middle and bottom shelves in notches of uprights; secure at back with screws, making sure the plant stand is level.

Painting

Give the stand a wash of diluted green, water-based paint and a coat of protective varnish. If it is for outdoor use, use acrylic paint.

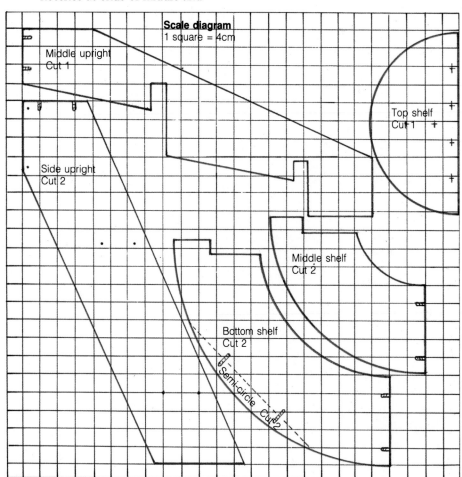

Scale diagram
1 square = 4cm

Middle upright
Cut 1

Side upright
Cut 2

Top shelf
Cut 1

Middle shelf
Cut 2

Bottom shelf
Cut 2

Semicircle Cut 2

Parquetry

*Paper-thin sheets of wood, known as veneer, form
the raw material for parquetry — a type of marquetry. With just
a few basic tools veneers can be overlaid on to a
base of cheaper, solid wood — such as a table top — using
techniques which offer unlimited scope for design.*

For centuries, craftsmen have used differently coloured woods and precious materials, such as ivory and tortoiseshell, to form beautiful patterns on furniture. The method, known as marquetry, involves either inlaying the materials in the surface of the furniture or forming a pieced pattern, which is then put on the furniture as a veneer. Marquetry patterns range from stylized geometric designs to elaborate and detailed pictorial scenes.

While marquetry is complicated and requires a lot of skill, parquetry — a form of marquetry — is an ideal starting point for those who want to try this craft. In parquetry the designs are traditionally simple, geometric patterns cut from thin veneers of wood. The wide range of thin veneers of wood available from DIY and hardware stores make this craft quite accessible.

Parquetry table

Use this attractive parquetry design to decorate an item of plain or shabby furniture. Different coloured veneers, thin enough to be cut with a strong knife, have been used to form the pattern. The instructions given are for a table measuring about 20in (50cm) in diameter.

You will need
◇ A solid wood table, about 20in
   (50cm) in diameter
◇ 20 pieces of wood veneer, 9 x 7in
   (23 x 18cm); 10 in a plain veneer
   and 10 in speckled maple
◇ 20 pieces of craft paper, 10 x 8in
   (25 x 20cm)
◇ Quick-drying wood glue
◇ Flat brush and a pencil
◇ Tracing paper and cardboard
◇ Craft knife or scalpel (a very
   sharp, fine blade is essential)
◇ Cutting board
◇ Small pot of mahogany wood filler
◇ Bottle of acetone

◇ Rags
◇ Liquid wax and polishing duster
◇ Large books or telephone
directories for pressing
◇ Coarse, medium and fine sand
paper

Method

1 Protect work area with paper. To prepare the surface of the table, remove any paint using acetone — work with windows open.

2 Enlarge the motif to fit table — this becomes master diagram. Transfer diagram to table top.

3 Using the brush, paint wood glue on to one side of each piece of veneer. Apply rectangles of paper to the pieces of veneer and place them, glued surfaces apart, under a pile of heavy books or telephone directories. Leave to dry under the press for 24 hours.

4 Trace the five triangles from master diagram; transfer triangles to cardboard and cut out. Place triangles on paper side of veneer; draw round edges with a pencil. Using a craft knife, cut out 12 of each triangle from plain veneer. Repeat for maple veneer.

5 Put parquetry pieces on top of traced motif. Working from

centre in circles, number back of each piece and its place on design. Make sure pieces fit together accurately, rejecting any that do not. Cut more if needed.

6 Remove parquetry pieces. Spread glue over centre of table; replace central pieces of veneer, making sure numbers match. Glue rest of table and continue in same way. The last circle will slightly overlap edge of the table.

7 Carefully turn table upside down. Pile books or weights on top; leave for at least 24 hours to allow glue to dry thoroughly. Trim then sand overlapping edges.

8 Apply a thin layer of mahogany filler over table surface. Sand with coarse, medium and then fine sand paper. Using a heat-resistant polish, wax and polish the table top, legs and feet four times.

Pattern guide for table top